Laura Hannemann
Hochschule Karlsruhe—University
of Applied Sciences
Karlsruhe, Germany

ISSN 2625-3577 ISSN 2625-3615 (electronic)
BestMasters
ISBN 978-3-658-50958-3 ISBN 978-3-658-50959-0 (eBook)
https://doi.org/10.1007/978-3-658-50959-0

This Springer Gabler imprint is published by the registered company Springer Fachmedien Wiesbaden GmbH, part of Springer Nature.
The registered company address is: Abraham-Lincoln-Str. 46, 65189 Wiesbaden, Germany

BestMasters

Mit **„BestMasters“** zeichnet Springer die besten Masterarbeiten aus, die an renommierten Hochschulen in Deutschland, Österreich und der Schweiz entstanden sind. Die mit Höchstnote ausgezeichneten Arbeiten wurden durch Gutachter zur Veröffentlichung empfohlen und behandeln aktuelle Themen aus unterschiedlichen Fachgebieten der Naturwissenschaften, Psychologie, Sozialwissenschaften, Technik und Wirtschaftswissenschaften. Die Reihe wendet sich an Praktiker und Wissenschaftler gleichermaßen und soll insbesondere auch Nachwuchswissenschaftlern Orientierung geben.

Springer awards **“BestMasters”** to the best master’s theses which have been completed at renowned Universities in Germany, Austria, and Switzerland. The studies received highest marks and were recommended for publication by supervisors. They address current issues from various fields of research in natural sciences, psychology, social sciences, technology, and economics. The series addresses practitioners as well as scientists and, in particular, offers guidance for early stage researchers.

Laura Hannemann

Integrating Marketing Analytics Approaches into B2B Lead Management

A Practical Guide for Process Optimization

Springer Gabler

Acknowledgments This master's thesis deals with an interdisciplinary, future-oriented, and practice-relevant topic at the intersection of marketing analytics, B2B lead management, and process optimization. Based on my previous professional experience with lead management from a sales point of view, I was very interested in examining this process from a marketing perspective and exploring its implications in a data-driven and process-oriented context.

I would like to take this opportunity to express my sincere gratitude to everyone who supported me during the writing process and on the path to publication. In addition to my family, friends, and fellow students, I would like to thank the participating experts. Their willingness to share not only their time but also their valuable experiences and insights was crucial to the practical relevance of this work.

Furthermore, I am particularly grateful to my supervisor, Prof. Dr. Markus Schwarz, for his continuous support, guidance, and expertise throughout the development of this thesis, as well as for his encouragement to publish the work. Further thanks go to my co-advisor, Prof. Fei-Fei Cheng.

I hope you enjoy reading.

Bonn
December 2025

Laura Hannemann

Competing Interests The author has no competing interests to declare that are relevant to the content of this manuscript.

Abstract

Despite the growing importance of acquiring new customers due to increased global competition, lead management processes in business-to-business (B2B) companies often remain ineffective. Marketing analytics offers opportunities to address common issues in lead generation, lead scoring, and lead nurturing through data insights. Simultaneously, it enables companies to measure the effectiveness of their lead management efforts. Nevertheless, the extent of data-driven decision-making varies in practice, and the academic literature on marketing analytics in B2B lead management remains fragmented.

This thesis bridges the gap by demonstrating how marketing analytics approaches can be integrated into B2B lead management to improve process effectiveness. By combining theoretical foundations with insights from expert interviews, the thesis identifies common challenges and corresponding analytics applications of varying complexity across the lead management process. This is supported by metrics and approaches to measuring effectiveness. The findings are combined in a practical guide that contains steps and recommendations for the integration of marketing analytics, along with relevant success factors. Even though no "one-size-fits-all" solution exists, B2B marketing professionals are offered actionable approaches considering different maturity levels.

Keywords: B2B Lead Management · Marketing Analytics · Lead Generation · Lead Scoring · Lead Nurturing · Marketing Automation · Customer Journey · Artificial Intelligence · Data-Driven Decision-Making · Effectiveness Measurement

Zusammenfassung

Trotz der zunehmenden Bedeutung der Neukundengewinnung aufgrund des verschärften globalen Wettbewerbs bleiben Lead-Management-Prozesse in Business-to-Business (B2B)-Unternehmen oft ineffektiv. Marketing Analytics bietet die Möglichkeit, häufige Probleme bei der Lead-Generierung, der Lead-Bewertung und der Lead-Pflege durch Dateneinblicke zu lösen. Gleichzeitig ermöglicht es Unternehmen, die Effektivität ihrer Lead-Management-Bemühungen zu messen. In der Praxis variiert das Ausmaß der datengetriebenen Entscheidungsfindung und die akademische Literatur zu Marketing Analytics im B2B-Lead-Management bleibt fragmentiert.

Die vorliegende Arbeit schließt diese Lücke, indem sie aufzeigt, wie Marketing Analytics-Ansätze in das B2B-Lead-Management integriert werden können, um die Effektivität der Prozesse zu verbessern. Durch die Kombination theoretischer Grundlagen mit Erkenntnissen aus Experteninterviews identifiziert die Arbeit häufige Herausforderungen und entsprechende Analytics-Anwendungen von unterschiedlicher Komplexität im Lead-Management-Prozess. Dies wird durch Metriken und Ansätze zur Messung der Effektivität unterstützt. Die Erkenntnisse werden in einem Praxisleitfaden vereint, der Schritte und Empfehlungen für die Integration von Marketing Analytics sowie relevante Erfolgsfaktoren enthält. Obwohl es keine „Einheitslösung" gibt, werden B2B-Marketingfachleuten umsetzbare Ansätze geboten, die unterschiedliche Reifegrade berücksichtigen.

Schlüsselwörter: B2B-Lead-Management · Marketing Analytics · Lead-Generierung · Lead-Bewertung · Lead-Pflege · Marketing Automation · Customer Journey · Künstliche Intelligenz · Datengetriebene Entscheidungsfindung · Effektivitätsmessung

Contents

Abbreviations

AI	Artificial Intelligence
B2B	Business-to-Business
B2C	Business-to-Consumer
BI	Business Intelligence
CRM	Customer Relationship Management
DACH region	Germany, Austria, and Switzerland
GDPR	General Data Protection Regulation
ICP	Ideal Customer Profile
KPI	Key Performance Indicator
MQL	Marketing Qualified Lead
PDCA	Plan, Do, Check, Act
ROI	Return on Investment
SAL	Sales Accepted Lead
SEA	Search Engine Advertising
SEO	Search Engine Optimization
SQL	Sales Qualified Lead
TAL	Telesales Accepted Lead

List of Figures

List of Tables

1 Introduction

This section introduces the research problem, the research questions, and the thesis structure.

1.1 Problem Statement and Research Relevance

According to Länsipuro & Karjaluoto (2021, p. 22), “ever-developing web and technological advancements present marketers with better approaches to measuring, optimizing, and automating marketing processes.” Therefore, marketing analytics plays an increasingly important role in marketing efforts (Länsipuro & Karjaluoto, 2021, p. 22). Data-driven approaches are also crucial in the digital transformation of lead management (Vossebein et al., 2024, p. 3). Successful lead management is an important endeavor for companies, as rising global competition requires them to continuously acquire new customers (Gebhardt & Gebhardt, 2019, p. 77). A study conducted in 2022 among 226 companies in the DACH region[1] (76% of which were B2B companies) highlighted the practical importance of lead management. Most respondents identified generating new leads as a crucial objective in marketing and sales, while lead scoring and nurturing were also considered important goals (Zumstein et al., 2023, pp. 10–16).

[1] DACH region refers to the German-speaking region of Europe, i.e., Germany, Austria, and Switzerland.

Supplementary Information The online version contains supplementary material available at https://doi.org/10.1007/978-3-658-50959-0_1.

L. Hannemann, *Integrating Marketing Analytics Approaches into B2B Lead Management*, BestMasters, https://doi.org/10.1007/978-3-658-50959-0_1

Lead management aims to guide potential customers through their purchasing journey to ultimately convert them into actual customers (Hannig, 2021, p. 244). Depending on internal responsibilities, companies can adopt a marketing- or sales-oriented perspective to lead management (Wenger, 2023, p. 494). In recent years, the role of marketing in lead management has expanded significantly, as customers increasingly use digital channels during the early stages of purchasing (Terho et al., 2023, p. 340). From a marketing-oriented perspective, lead management typically comprises the stages of lead generation, qualification and scoring, and nurturing, concluding with the handover of qualified leads to sales (Huttelmaier & Heigl, 2023, p. 299; Järvinen & Taiminen, 2016, pp. 170–173). As Ohiomah et al. (2016, p. 5) emphasize, "well-organized lead management is an important part of marketing effectiveness." Lead management success is often measured from an effectiveness perspective, mainly referring to the quantity and quality of leads and conversion rates (Wenger, 2023, p. 494). Although not a focus of this thesis, efficiency aspects such as the cost to acquire and convert a lead also contribute to lead management performance (Dach, 2023, pp. 40–41).

Espadinha-Cruz et al. (2021, p. 1) point out that the lead management process frequently remains ineffective, and companies encounter various challenges. These range from inadequately defined processes, misalignment between marketing and sales, and missing system integrations to insufficient data use (Espadinha-Cruz et al., 2021, pp. 1–2; Vossebein et al., 2024, pp. 1–3). This often leads to inadequate lead qualification and engagement, with decisions relying on intuition and experience rather than data (Gasser & Mäder, 2022, pp. 99–100; Wu et al., 2024a, p. 5). The results are often insufficient lead quality, low conversion rates, and missed opportunities (Espadinha-Cruz et al., 2021, pp. 1–2).

Integrating marketing analytics approaches into lead management can help address common issues (Rackley, 2015, p. 110). It provides companies with data-driven insights that help identify and better understand potential customers, prioritize leads with high potential, and personalize engagement strategies (Albrecht & Schlüter, 2022, p. 210; Rosário & Dias, 2023, pp. 9–10). Marketing analytics involves collecting, managing, and analyzing marketing data to generate insights that help improve decision-making and performance (Wedel & Kannan, 2016, pp. 97–98). Therefore, the concept encompasses both learning from data and measuring performance, allowing companies to make data-driven decisions and improve outcomes (Mero et al., 2020, pp. 218–220). Despite its potential, the extent to which companies leverage marketing analytics for decision-making varies significantly (Agag et al., 2024, p. 3). In this context, many marketers remain dissatisfied with the outcomes of their analytics initiatives, frequently causing a reluctance to rely on data insights for decision-making (Gartner, 2020).

Despite promising use cases in the realm of predictive analytics and Artificial Intelligence (AI), recent studies indicate that the implementation of these advanced analytics approaches in B2B lead management is limited, and many companies are still facing issues related to a lack of automation (Zumstein et al., 2024, p. 40). However, this thesis will show that companies can start with more basic methods to advance data-driven strategies in lead management. To the best of the author's knowledge, few theoretical publications to date address the application of marketing analytics to business-to-business (B2B)[2] lead management, and academic research in the field remains fragmented. Contributions frequently focus on individual use cases or highly advanced approaches (e.g., Cogan & Orgis, 2021), cover only individual stages of the lead management process (e.g., Gebhardt & Gebhardt, 2019), or are not explicitly linked to B2B settings (e.g., Agag et al., 2024). However, B2B markets are characterized by more complex offerings, higher order values, longer decision-making processes involving multiple stakeholders, and a limited availability and accessibility of data compared to B2C settings (Lilien, 2016, p. 545; Reklaitis & Pileliene, 2019, pp. 76–77). These unique characteristics require a tailored approach to B2B lead management (Wenger, 2023, p. 487). Therefore, this thesis seeks to bridge the academic and practical gap by developing an actionable guide for B2B companies on how marketing analytics can be integrated into B2B lead management to improve process effectiveness. As mentioned, this ultimately refers to improving lead quantity, quality and conversion rates. Based on the understanding of marketing analytics described previously, two dimensions are considered (Mero et al., 2020, pp. 218–220):

- Learning from data: Using data insights (e.g., demographic, behavioral) to improve the lead management process stages, focusing on marketing analytics applications in lead generation, lead scoring, and lead nurturing.
- Measuring performance: Determining metrics (e.g., conversion rates) and approaches (e.g., funnel performance management) to measure lead management effectiveness.

[2] Unlike business-to-consumer (B2C) companies that sell to individual consumers, business-to-business (B2B) companies offer their products and services to other businesses (Reklaitis & Pileliene, 2019, p. 76).

Based on common challenges, this thesis presents marketing analytics applications that companies can realistically adopt. Due to the limited relevance in practice, highly statistical or algorithmic approaches related to predictive analytics and AI are not examined in detail. However, possibilities are presented to illustrate the current state of research and future directions.

1.2 Research Objectives and Scope

To address the previously mentioned gap, this thesis combines theoretical foundations with empirical findings from expert interviews. The primary objective is to develop a practical guide for integrating marketing analytics approaches into B2B lead management to enhance process effectiveness. This guide contains concrete steps and recommendations that enable marketing professionals in B2B companies of various sizes and industries to improve the outcomes of their data-driven lead management processes. It highlights prerequisites and success factors for integration, provides clear steps for marketing analytics applications at different stages of the lead management process, and offers possibilities for measuring effectiveness.

The central research question is: *RQ: How can marketing analytics approaches be integrated into B2B lead management to make processes more effective?*

To enable a structured analysis of the research question, two sub-questions are derived:

- *SQ1: Which key challenges and bottlenecks hinder effectiveness in B2B lead management, and how can insights from marketing analytics optimize specific stages of the process?*
- *SQ2: Which metrics and success factors are required for integrating marketing analytics approaches into B2B lead management processes?*

Appendix 1 in the Electronic Supplementary Material shows how these questions will be addressed in the thesis structure.

For a targeted analysis, the scope of the thesis is limited. Although in some organizations, lead management is the sole responsibility of sales, this thesis is deliberately limited to scenarios in which marketing plays or will play an active role. The analysis focuses on the tasks of marketing in the lead management process up to the handover to sales. Following Vossebein et al. (2024, pp. 7–8), the thesis does not cover sales processes after the lead handover, such as the negotiation and after-sales phase. The role of sales is mainly examined in the context of marketing-sales alignment and as a source of feedback for evaluating lead quality. Although process efficiency is considered to the extent that it impacts effectiveness, the focus is on effectiveness-oriented improvements. Additionally, this thesis discusses lead management for acquiring new customers rather than maintaining existing customer relationships. While issues related to data are included, the thesis does not investigate operational and legal issues related to data collection and management in depth.

1.3 Methodological Approach and Structure

This thesis starts by creating the conceptual framework as a basis for the empirical research. The first part covers an overview of lead management in B2B companies, including definitions, the marketing and sales funnel, the connection to the B2B customer journey, and the lead management process stages. In this context, a glance at common challenges and success factors in B2B lead management is provided. Subsequently, the fundamentals of marketing analytics are presented and general prerequisites for its deployment are outlined. This is followed by a discussion of marketing analytics applications of varying complexity that can be used to tackle common challenges in the lead management process stages. Finally, there is a chapter on measuring the effectiveness of lead management. The literature review for the conceptual framework includes journal articles, monographs, and industry contributions. This variety is needed to ensure both academic depth and practical applicability.

The next section of the thesis focuses on the empirical research. The chosen methodology is expert interviews, a frequently used method for collecting qualitative data (Helfferich, 2022, pp. 887–888). Expert interviews are the preferred method for this thesis as they provide in-depth, practice-oriented insights that cannot be obtained from literature or quantitative methods (Bogner et al., 2014, pp. 1–3). Given the identified gap, this approach is particularly valuable for exploring the various dimensions of the research problem. The interviews are conducted with marketing professionals working for B2B companies of various sizes and across different industries, with a focus on decision-makers involved in lead management processes. An interview with an expert working for a B2B marketing agency is used to provide an external perspective. The interviews are evaluated using content-structuring qualitative content analysis to categorize and analyze the data (Kuckartz & Rädiker, 2024, p. 132). The goal is to understand the lead management processes in B2B companies and the application of marketing analytics. This also includes factors that contribute to the successful implementation of such approaches. In the final part of the thesis, recommendations for the practical guide are derived from the theoretical insights and empirical findings.

German direct quotations throughout the thesis were translated using the DeepL translation service (DeepL, n. d.).

Conceptual Framework 2

The theoretical section of the thesis describes the fundamentals of B2B lead management and marketing analytics, ultimately combining these concepts in Sect. 2.3.

2.1 Lead Management in B2B Companies

This section discusses the definition and foundations of lead management, the marketing and sales funnel, and the connection to the B2B customer journey. Next, the stages of the lead management process are introduced, along with relevant supporting technologies. Common challenges and bottlenecks in B2B lead management are discussed at the end of the section.

2.1.1 Definition and Foundations

There is no generally accepted definition of lead management in the literature (Vossebein et al., 2024, p. 5; Wenger, 2023, p. 494). In a broad sense, lead management involves "measures that a company takes to turn potential buyers or interested parties into actual buyers" (Seebacher, 2023, p. 77). Wenger (2023, p. 494) offers a more detailed definition: "Lead management is the methodology, process, and software to generate, nurture, and qualify leads using sales and marketing strategies." This definition serves as a basis for the thesis, as it explicitly integrates marketing and sales perspectives and addresses core stages of lead management (Sect. 2.1.3). According to Monat (2011, p. 179), a lead is

L. Hannemann, *Integrating Marketing Analytics Approaches into B2B Lead Management*, BestMasters, https://doi.org/10.1007/978-3-658-50959-0_2

a "recorded expressed interest in the company's goods or services." Lead management provides a structured approach to capturing and handling data on the interest of potential customers in a company's offerings (Deszczyński, 2016, p. 1). It enables tailored customer acquisition through the precise selection of leads and strategies to address individual needs (Espadinha-Cruz et al., 2021, p. 1).

Depending on the organization, the responsibilities for lead management are divided between marketing and sales. The latter can refer to both outside and inside sales (Terho et al., 2023, pp. 337–338; Wu et al., 2024b, pp. 69–70). As mentioned, this thesis focuses on scenarios in which marketing plays a key role. However, several authors highlight the need to move beyond a departmental approach, as effective lead management requires collaboration across functions (Steuernagel, 2021, p. 23; Vossebein et al., 2024, p. 48). In addition, structured lead management promotes transparency in marketing and sales and enables the assessment of marketing's impact on a company's success (Gasser & Mäder, 2022, p. 27).

According to Wenger (2023, p. 502), companies differ in their lead management maturity. This includes the extent to which processes are defined and standardized, as well as the relationship status between marketing and sales. As they mature, companies move toward systematic lead management with greater integration of marketing and sales and dedicated software support. As Fig. 2.1 shows, four stages are distinguished (Wenger, 2023, pp. 502–504):

- No lead management: No active management of leads, direct generation of sales opportunities by sales, undefined marketing-sales relationship.
- Defined lead management terms: Basic understanding and definitions, process not fully developed, no software support, defined marketing-sales relationship.
- Defined lead management process: Clear lead qualification levels and process, software support, aligned marketing-sales relationship.
- Dedicated lead management department: Clear responsibilities, terminology, shared goals, well-integrated software, integrated marketing-sales relationship.

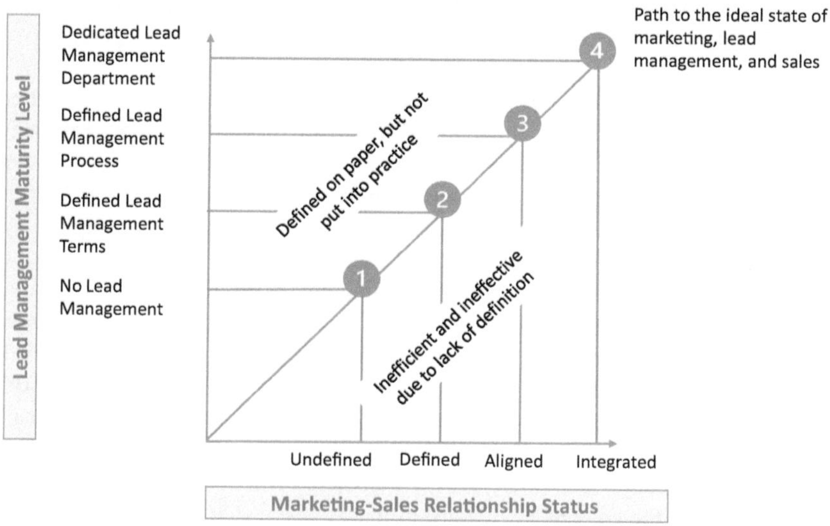

Fig. 2.1 Lead Management Maturity Model. (Source: Reproduced and translated from Wenger (2023, p. 502))

However, Wenger's model remains limited in terms of technological requirements, data availability, and the degree of automation.

2.1.2 Marketing and Sales Funnel and B2B Customer Journey

Having covered the foundations of lead management, this section focuses on the concepts of the marketing and sales funnel and the customer journey. The traditional sales funnel depicts the process of systematically reducing a company's numerous potential buyers to a final set of customers. At each stage, the number of contacts decreases while their purchase probability progressively improves (Cooper & Budd, 2007, p. 176; D'Haen & Van den Poel, 2013, p. 545). As digital resources play an increasing role in early purchase decisions, the importance of marketing in lead management has become critical (Steuernagel, 2021, p. 23; Terho et al., 2023, p. 340). Therefore, several scholars have developed integrated funnel models that account for interactions between sales and marketing (e.g., Gebhardt, 2023, p. 70; Järvinen & Taiminen, 2016, p. 170; Terho et al., 2023,

p. 339). This thesis presents Gebhardt's framework due to its detailed lead qualification levels and focus on B2B lead management but supports it with perspectives from other authors.

The first stage involves *Open Leads*, contacts that have not yet been qualified or prioritized (Gebhardt & Gebhardt, 2019, p. 78). In the next step, *Marketing Qualified Leads (MQLs)* are identified, i.e., contacts who match the target group and have a certain likelihood of making a purchase. They are qualified and prioritized accordingly, as determined through lead scoring and lead nurturing. Leads that meet the predefined threshold of engagement and qualification are passed to sales (Gebhardt, 2023, p. 70; Järvinen & Taiminen, 2016, pp. 171–172).

Once leads reach the sales department, they are evaluated to ensure they meet maturity criteria. MQLs that have been reviewed and accepted by sales as worth pursuing are categorized as *Sales Accepted Leads (SALs)* (Hannig, 2021, p. 505; Huttelmaier & Heigl, 2023, p. 301). This step marks the handover from marketing to sales and requires a joint definition of sales maturity (Gebhardt, 2023, p. 70). In this context, leads are typically transferred from the marketing automation platform to the customer relationship management (CRM) system, ensuring IT integration (Järvinen & Taiminen, 2016, p. 172). Leads that fulfill further criteria and are actively pursued by sales are referred to as *Sales Qualified Leads (SQLs)* (Wenger, 2023, p. 492). The last stages focus on converting SQLs with concrete sales potential (*Opportunities*) into buying customers (*Orders*) through sales negotiations (Gebhardt, 2023, p. 71).

Leads can re-enter the funnel at different stages based on re-engagement or additional qualification (Järvinen & Taiminen, 2016, p. 172). Even though not a focus of this thesis, the funnel can also be used for managing existing customer relationships (Gebhardt, 2023, p. 71; Järvinen & Taiminen, 2016, p. 166).

The shape, number of stages, and points at which leads are transferred from marketing to sales vary between funnel frameworks (Huttelmaier & Heigl, 2023, pp. 301–302; Järvinen & Taiminen, 2016, p. 166). Some models omit the SAL stage, with lead handover occurring directly from MQL to SQL (e.g., Gebhardt & Gebhardt, 2019, p. 78). In other models, different terminology is used, such as distinguishing between cold, warm, and hot leads (e.g., Wenger, 2023, p. 493). Therefore, businesses need to ensure clear internal definitions and criteria for each lead qualification level (Huttelmaier & Heigl, 2023, p. 300).

Although it offers a structured framework for lead qualification, the marketing and sales funnel is occasionally criticized for being too rigid. It is argued that the model does not accurately reflect the complexity of B2B decision-making (Gasser & Mäder, 2022, pp. 20–21). Because there are usually numerous stakeholders involved, the B2B customer journey does not follow a linear sequence but instead comprises multiple paths (Gasser & Mäder, 2022, p. 21; Maechler et al., 2017, p. 3). Consequently, some scholars advocate the customer journey as a more holistic, iterative and flexible alternative to the funnel model (Gasser & Mäder, 2022, p. 2). According to Hannig (2021, p. 246), the customer journey is the path a potential customer follows in the direction of a purchase and includes all interactions with a company, brand, or offering across touchpoints and channels. Instead of favoring one concept over the other, this thesis combines insights from both the marketing and sales funnel and the B2B customer journey.

Several studies recognize that the B2B customer journey is becoming increasingly digital (e.g., Lundin & Kindström, 2023; Rustholkarhu et al., 2022). In the past, marketing often focused on generating leads and then quickly passing them to sales. However, since modern buyers rely more on digital resources, they often engage less with sales in the early purchasing stages (Świeczak & Łukowski, 2016, pp. 110–111). Meanwhile, the role of marketing has expanded to ensure leads are continuously engaged and nurtured until purchase (Andersen et al., 2018, pp. 1–2). To support this shift and strengthen marketing-driven lead conversion, "companies need to invest in technology, data, and analytics to improve insights into customer buying behavior and help provide more relevant, personalized experiences" (Andersen et al., 2018, p. 4).

2.1.3 Lead Management Process Stages

Research in various trade journals, monographs, and industry publications has confirmed that there is no universal lead management process. Nevertheless, lead generation, scoring, nurturing, and handover are commonly identified as core components (Gasser & Mäder, 2022, p. 131; Huttelmaier & Heigl, 2023, p. 299; Järvinen & Taiminen, 2016, pp. 164–165). However, views differ on how to position lead qualification. Some scholars place qualification after lead generation (e.g., Vossebein et al., 2024, pp. 21–22), and others introduce it only after lead scoring and nurturing (e.g., Wenger, 2023, p. 495). This suggests that qualification is an iterative process. For practical purposes, this thesis presents lead qualification alongside scoring, as they are closely interrelated (Stevens, 2012, pp. 139–153). However, the recurring nature of lead qualification is acknowledged. Throughout the lead management process, seamless data access and continuous exchange of information are crucial (Vossebein et al., 2024, p. 38).

Based on these considerations, Fig. 2.2 shows the B2B lead management process stages.

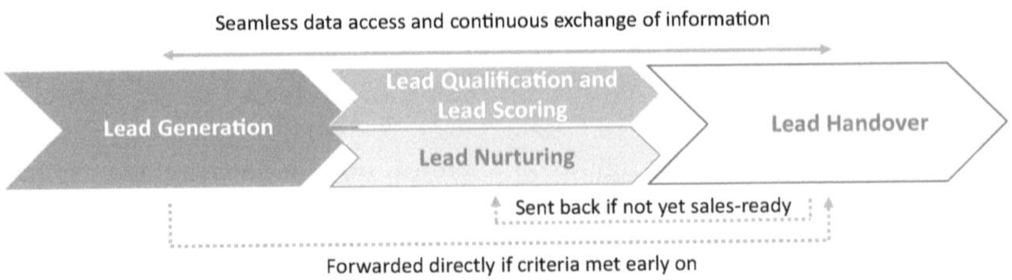

Fig. 2.2 Stages of the B2B Lead Management Process. (Source: Adapted from Huttelmaier & Heigl (2023, p. 299))

The process is not linear, as leads may be downgraded or, if qualification criteria are met early, passed to sales directly after lead generation (Järvinen & Taiminen, 2016, p. 171), as illustrated by the dashed lines in Fig. 2.2. The following section gives an overview of the process flow and main activities to build the foundation for applying marketing analytics in Sect. 2.3.

Lead Generation

Lead generation involves identifying and targeting potential customers who are interested in a company's offerings (Świeczak & Łukowski, 2016, p. 109). Clearly defined target groups form the basis of lead generation and improve the understanding of potential customers' needs (Beck, 2025, pp. 51–53; Gebhardt & Gebhardt, 2019, p. 77), as discussed in Sect. 2.3.1.

The potential customer, who at this point is merely a contact, i.e., a "rudimentarily known person from the target group," interacts with various online or offline channels (Wenger, 2023, p. 495). Lead generation typically distinguishes between inbound and outbound marketing. Inbound marketing attracts potential customers through valuable and engaging content (Dach, 2023, pp. 8–9). Therefore, their interest must be piqued in a way that encourages them to voluntarily provide contact details, such as their email address (N. Schuster, 2022, p. 90). If companies need to follow data protection regulations, they must obtain opt-in (consent to be contacted) and provide a privacy policy (N. Schuster, 2022, p. 107). Content marketing is an important inbound approach that provides digital content, such as whitepapers, tailored to the interests of the target group (Järvinen & Taiminen, 2016, pp. 164–170). This content is often gated, which means that the contact receives access in exchange for providing their details via designated forms (Gasser & Mäder, 2022, p. 75). The specific contact data collected depends on the company's definition of a lead (Jadli et al., 2023, p. 1281). Apart from content marketing, landing pages, social media, search engine advertising (SEA) and search engine optimization (SEO) are common methods for generating leads (Vossebein et al., 2024, pp. 26–27).

Outbound marketing, typically associated with cold calling, refers to companies directly approaching prospective customers. This, for example, involves purchasing contact lists, organizing trade fairs, or sending mass mailings (Dach, 2023, pp. 7–9). Although companies are increasingly focusing on inbound strategies (Hannig, 2021, p. 246), trade fairs and events remain highly relevant in lead generation (Zumstein et al., 2024, pp. 13–14). Ultimately, "effective lead generation [...] is based on understanding which of the tactics will generate the most beneficial leads for the company" (Świeczak & Łukowski, 2016, p. 131).

Lead Qualification and Scoring

Following lead generation, companies assess if a lead meets the necessary criteria to advance in the customer journey and has the potential to convert into a customer (Gasser & Mäder, 2022, p. 116). Lead qualification is an important step in effectively turning leads into customers (Espadinha-Cruz et al., 2021, p. 3). Often, marketing is responsible for lead qualification before handover, and sales qualifies the leads further after having received them from marketing (Steuernagel, 2021, pp. 24–28). To create an accurate profile, marketing often enriches data about the individual or the company with further insights, such as background information about the person or the company's product portfolio (Vossebein et al., 2024, pp. 28–30). To create a basis for processing leads, they are evaluated based on different factors. Depending on how well leads match the qualification criteria, they can either be processed further in lead nurturing or forwarded directly to sales. As there are no general guidelines, companies must derive their own criteria for evaluating lead quality (Vossebein et al., 2024, pp. 31–32).

Lead scoring is a central element of lead qualification and an "effective and efficient way of measuring the quality of leads" (Wu et al., 2024b, p. 69). It allows companies to evaluate and prioritize leads based on their likelihood to convert into customers (Wu et al., 2024b, p. 74). To ensure that high-quality leads are approached and sales losses are avoided, only leads with sufficient potential are handed over to sales (Monat, 2011, p. 192; Paschen et al., 2020, pp. 406–408). Companies can use different lead scoring models depending on the availability of data (González-Flores et al., 2025, pp. 5–6), as discussed in Sect. 2.3.2.

After handover, leads are usually qualified further through a direct interaction with the sales representative (Gasser & Mäder, 2022, p. 134). However, since this thesis focuses on lead management up to the lead handover, qualification on the sales side is not described.

Lead Nurturing

As shown in Fig. 2.2, lead nurturing usually occurs in parallel with lead scoring. Marketing efforts employed during the nurturing process help increase the lead score, while lead scoring makes the nurturing process measurable (Wenger, 2023, pp. 496–497). Leads are not always ready to buy immediately after they have been generated. In this context, lead nurturing helps to develop them further and move them closer to a purchase decision. Lead nurturing aims to build and maintain a trusting relationship with leads and gradually increase their interest until they are ready to be transferred to sales (Järvinen & Taiminen, 2016, p. 167). Therefore, lead nurturing often includes personalized communication (Paschen et al., 2020, p. 408). At this point, a personalized approach is possible because companies already have more information about the lead (Wenger, 2023, pp. 497–498), as shown in Sect. 2.3.3.

Lead nurturing often involves email marketing campaigns, invitations to events, or webinars (Dach, 2023, p. 35). Several authors agree that email marketing is an important nurturing approach (Dach, 2023, p. 35; Philipp, 2021, p. 205). Additionally, lead nurturing is often supported by marketing automation software and concludes with the transfer of leads to sales when they meet defined scoring thresholds (Järvinen & Taiminen, 2016, pp. 170–171).

Lead Handover

Once they have been forwarded to sales, leads are assigned to the appropriate sales channel or sales representative (Huttelmaier & Heigl, 2023, p. 300). This is also referred to as lead routing (Hannig, 2021, p. 505). In some companies, MQLs must be formally reviewed and accepted by sales. This requires clear definitions of a high-quality lead (Klaus, 2023, p. 446). The sales team uses these criteria to determine whether to accept the lead and make it an SAL or return it to marketing for additional nurturing (Huttelmaier & Heigl, 2023, pp. 301–302). Companies can establish responsibilities and timelines for lead acceptance and follow-up through service-level agreements between marketing and sales (Klaus, 2023, p. 446).

Table 2.1 summarizes the stages of the lead management process as described in this chapter.

Table 2.1 Overview of Lead Management Process Stages

Process Element	Purpose	Main Activities	Responsibility
Lead Generation	Identify and target the right potential customers	• Define the target group • Apply inbound and outbound marketing strategies • Capture contact details	Marketing
Lead Qualification and Scoring	Qualify and prioritize leads for sales	• Qualify leads and enrich information • Leverage lead scoring • Qualify leads further after handover	Marketing (Sales after handover)
Lead Nurturing	Develop leads toward sales readiness	• Engage leads with personalized communication • Enrich lead profiles	Marketing
Lead Handover	Transfer MQLs to sales for direct engagement	• Formalize lead acceptance • Define responsibilities with service-level agreements	Marketing and Sales

Source: Own depiction

2.1.4 Technological Infrastructure for Lead Management

Having provided an overview of the lead management process stages, this chapter describes systems and tools that can support the process. According to Terho et al. (2023, p. 348), "integrated MA [Marketing Automation] and CRM systems form the technological backbone of contemporary lead management." As described below, marketing automation and CRM systems offer different features to facilitate lead management activities.

CRM systems are widely used in the DACH region (Heinzelbecker, 2021, p. 136) and have been identified as the most crucial marketing technology in a 2023 study among B2B and B2C companies (Zumstein et al., 2023, p. 14). These systems gather and store customer and transaction data to create holistic customer profiles (Khodakarami & Chan, 2014, p. 27), including demographic information, purchasing behavior, and communication preferences (von Focht, 2022, p. 93). While traditional CRM systems were largely sales-focused, modern platforms offer expanded lead management capabilities and include marketing functions

(Heinzelbecker, 2021, pp. 135–140). Marketing and sales professionals can target potential customers with the help of data stored in CRM systems and conduct different analyses using integrated analytics capabilities (von Focht, 2022, p. 93). There are numerous vendors of CRM software, including Microsoft Dynamics CRM, Salesforce, and SAP CRM (Heinzelbecker, 2021, p. 140).

According to Mero (2020, p. 213), marketing automation is a "technology leveraged to improve the effectiveness and efficacy of marketing operations via automated, personalized, and analytics-driven activities." Marketing automation supports core functions of lead management (Silva et al., 2021, p. 148) by offering automated support for lead generation, scoring, nurturing, and routing (Rougemont & Terstiege, 2022, pp. 119–120). An important capability of marketing automation is the collection and analysis of information about the lead's behavior and interests, which enables targeted guidance throughout the customer journey by delivering relevant content (Järvinen & Taiminen, 2016, pp. 164–165). Therefore, according to Rackley (2015, p. 107), marketing automation is an important enabler for marketing analytics. Marketing automation captures leads, such as when an individual enters their email address in an online form. A user profile is created, which is enriched with information collected from the individual's click, read, and interaction behavior (Järvinen & Taiminen, 2016, pp. 170–172). Based on the acquired data, personalized and relevant information can be provided to potential customers as part of lead nurturing. Integrated lead scoring models facilitate the evaluation and prioritization of leads (Rougemont & Terstiege, 2022, pp. 117–119).

Numerous providers of marketing automation solutions offer specialized features for different needs (K. Nair & Gupta, 2021, p. 325). Small businesses often use inexpensive tools, such as Mailchimp or Mautic, while large companies frequently utilize enterprise platforms, for example, from HubSpot, Salesforce, SAP, or Microsoft. The most frequently used applications for marketing automation in the DACH region include HubSpot, Mailchimp, and Salesforce Pardot (Zumstein et al., 2023, p. 22). In the above-mentioned study, 75% of respondents considered marketing automation an important technology, which represented a significant increase compared to previous years. The authors of the study concluded that companies in the DACH region use marketing automation more frequently (Zumstein et al., 2023, pp. 14–15). A similar trend was observed in a study conducted in 2022 (Huttelmaier et al., 2022, p. 11).

According to Redding (2015, p. 261), CRM systems and marketing automation platforms "can provide the glue that helps align sales and marketing in B2B organizations." The boundaries between the technologies have become fluid, as vendors from both areas expand their offerings (Redding, 2015, p. 2). For instance, vendors like HubSpot and Salesforce offer both a CRM and marketing automation function (Brummer, 2024; Salesforce, n. d.).

2.1.5 Common Challenges and Success Factors

The previous chapters have presented numerous possibilities for process design and technology support. Nevertheless, as indicated in the introduction, lead management processes often remain ineffective (Espadinha-Cruz et al., 2021, p. 1). Therefore, this section deals with common challenges and success factors. Since various aspects are mentioned in the literature, no exhaustive list is provided. Vossebein et al. (2024, p. 14) recommend considering three dimensions: processes, people, and data. Given the importance of the technological infrastructure as described previously, technological factors are incorporated into the data dimension.

Process Dimension

As mentioned in Sect. 2.1.1, there are various levels of maturity in lead management that indicate differences in process definition and standardization. A common problem is that lead management processes and responsibilities are not adequately defined. However, this is a fundamental prerequisite (Vossebein et al., 2024, p. 14). Krieger (2021, p. 153) agrees that clear structures must be established to enable review and continuous adjustment of the process. Companies should only introduce IT support based on clearly defined processes. In addition, automation is recommended if the number of leads is large (Vossebein et al., 2024, p. 48).

Issues can occur at all stages of the lead management process. They should be identified to prevent reduced engagement or the loss of leads. Data analysis can help reveal bottlenecks and derive optimization measures (Zumstein et al., 2024, p. 42). The following section provides a brief overview of potential challenges at different process stages. Sect. 2.3 will illustrate how marketing analytics can help address those.

Often, the main issue for companies does not lie in generating enough leads (Beco & Zeren, 2023, p. 351). Still, they might fail to target the right potential customers through content or campaigns (Zumstein et al., 2024, p. 41). Thus, it is crucial to understand and identify the right target audience, as described in Sect. 2.3.1.

As Ohiomah et al. (2019, p. 163) argue, poorly managed leads can undermine the impact of otherwise effective marketing campaigns. A significant factor is frequently the insufficient quality of leads passed on to sales, which may result in low conversions (Wu et al., 2024b, p. 70). Many companies do not evaluate leads at all, do so manually, or use simple criteria (Zumstein et al., 2024, p. 17). Therefore, lead qualification often relies on personal experience and intuition rather than data (D'Haen et al., 2016, p. 69; Wu et al., 2024a, p. 5). As shown in Sect. 2.3.2, lead scoring can ensure that only promising leads are passed to sales.

Even high-potential leads will eventually be lost if companies fail to identify and address their needs. With rising expectations for personalized experiences, companies need to engage potential buyers in a meaningful way (Espadinha-Cruz et al., 2021, p. 2). However, many organizations still nurture their leads manually, without a consistent strategy, or not at all (Gasser & Mäder, 2022, pp. 99–100). Consequently, successful long-term communication with leads is often prevented (Fili et al., 2025, pp. 140–141). Therefore, as described in Sect. 2.3.3, effectively engaging potential customers over time is essential.

People Dimension

Another recurring theme in the literature is the lack of alignment between marketing and sales (Andersen et al., 2018, p. 3; Hannig, 2021, p. 252). In particular, unclear responsibilities and criteria can result in mutual blame (Kotler et al., 2006, p. 11; Steuernagel, 2021, p. 24). Ohiomah et al. (2016, p. 5) emphasize that lead management must ensure "that all generated and qualified leads are pursued by sales," as B2B organizations typically incur higher costs per lead generated than B2C companies. Nevertheless, the sales department is often criticized for not following up on a significant proportion of leads generated by marketing, a phenomenon known as the "sales lead black hole" (Sabnis et al., 2013, p. 52). At the same time, sales frequently complain about the quality of marketing-generated leads (Oliva, 2006, p. 397). This suggests that trust-based cooperation between marketing and sales is a crucial success factor in lead management, including clearly defined goals, process steps, and responsibilities (Terho et al., 2022, pp. 306–307). Qualification criteria for a sales-ready lead should be developed jointly by marketing and sales (Järvinen & Taiminen, 2016, p. 172). Further, sales should provide feedback on every forwarded lead in a timely manner (Huttelmaier & Heigl, 2023, p. 309).

Data and Technology Dimension

Since lead management depends on high-quality data, the completeness and accuracy of information are crucial. Yet, a lack of data, insufficient data quality, or inadequate use of existing data frequently hinder progress (D'Haen et al., 2016, p. 69; Espadinha-Cruz et al., 2021, p. 3). The inadequate use of existing data often stems from incomplete or outdated data sets in CRM systems, as data is not consistently maintained and updated. This can result in silos, where data is distributed across departments, impairing data quality (Gasser & Mäder, 2022, pp. 46–47). Therefore, the literature often advocates a "single source of truth" to enable centralized data and enhanced insights throughout the customer journey (Andersen et al., 2018, p. 5; Gasser & Mäder, 2022, p. 47). In addition, companies should continuously validate lead data to detect irregularities or quality issues (Espadinha-Cruz et al., 2021, pp. 4–5).

Additionally, companies may be required to comply with the General Data Protection Regulation (GDPR) of the European Union, which mandates transparency in data collection and secure data management practices (General Secretariat of the Council, n. d.). This, for example, includes obtaining consent for data processing (Gasser & Mäder, 2022, pp. 28–30).

According to Krieger (2021, p. 153), "lead management can only be fully effective when marketing technologies and systems are optimally coordinated, and a permanent flow of data is guaranteed." Thus, the implementation and seamless integration of software solutions are crucial. This particularly refers to CRM systems and marketing automation platforms (Krieger, 2021, p. 153). Apart from ensuring continuous data flow, their integration helps to establish a better "picture of customer behavior and marketing outcomes" (Mero et al., 2020, p. 218). System integration enables end-to-end tracking of the lead's journey from initial contact to conversion and helps to determine the contribution made to revenue by measures, content, or processes (Körner, 2021, p. 76). However, in practice, missing interfaces between CRM systems and marketing automation frequently remain an issue (Cogan & Orgis, 2021, p. 221).

2.2 Fundamentals of Marketing Analytics

After laying the foundations for the lead management process in the previous chapter, this section explores the fundamentals of marketing analytics, including the concept and scope, as well as the general prerequisites for its deployment. This is necessary to create an understanding for the application of marketing analytics in lead management in Sect. 2.3.

2.2.1 Concept and Scope

As companies generate and gather vast volumes of data, the need for data-driven decision support grows (Nygård & Mezei, 2020, p. 1439). Data can be defined as "a collection of facts, numbers, words, observations, or other useful information" that is transformed into actionable insights through data processing and analysis (IBM, 2024). According to a recent report, the importance of data to inform marketing strategies is steadily increasing. Among the advantages of data-driven efforts are better reaching target audiences, increasing the return on investment (ROI) of marketing activities, and enabling effective media mixes (HubSpot, 2025, p. 18).

Delen & Zolbanin (2018, p. 188) emphasize that there is no consensus on the scope and nature of the term analytics. According to them, analytics encompasses all applications of data that enhance decision-making and improve organizational performance (Delen & Zolbanin, 2018, pp. 187–188). Similarly, marketing analytics, a domain of business analytics, lacks a uniform definition (Iacobucci et al., 2019, p. 154; Kurtzke & Setkute, 2021, p. 3). In line with the understanding by Delen & Zolbanin and as outlined in the introduction, marketing analytics involves applying marketing data to generate insights for decision-making and performance optimization (Agag et al., 2024, p. 1; Wedel & Kannan, 2016, pp. 97–98). Marketing analytics helps companies move from purely intuitive and experience-based decisions to more data-driven decision-making (Rackley, 2015, p. 40). In this context, data-driven decision-making is referred to as "making informed decisions based on data and analytics rather than relying on personal intuition or guesswork" (Rosário & Dias, 2023, p. 11).

According to Albrecht & Schlüter (2022, p. 197), even though data enables evidence-based decisions, many marketing decisions are still dominated by "gut feeling." In contrast, Halfmann (2022, p. 3) states that gut feeling in marketing has "long since [...] been replaced by a strong focus on facts and figures." This suggests that the extent to which companies apply data-driven decision-making in practice remains unclear (Länsipuro & Karjaluoto, 2021, p. 22).

Beyond decision support, marketing analytics offers deeper insights into customer journeys (Basu et al., 2023, p. 2588). This is critical in B2B markets, where buyers expect customized interactions along increasingly digitized and self-directed journeys (Andersen et al., 2017, pp. 1–3). The goal is to better engage potential customers while achieving improved conversion and revenue outcomes (Rosário & Dias, 2023, p. 7).

To understand how marketing analytics can improve decision-making, it is helpful to distinguish between different levels of analytical sophistication. As mentioned, this thesis does not deal with advanced analytics in depth. Nevertheless, a brief overview is helpful to present the current state of research and set the stage for later comparisons. In the literature, a distinction is commonly made between descriptive, predictive, and prescriptive analytics (Delen & Demirkan, 2013, p. 361; Lepenioti et al., 2020, p. 57).[1]

Descriptive analytics focuses on understanding "what happened" by interpreting historical data (Delen & Zolbanin, 2018, p. 188). Predictive analytics describes "what will happen" (Delen & Zolbanin, 2018, p. 189) and applies statistical and mathematical methods to forecast future outcomes (Delen & Demirkan, 2013, p. 361). Prescriptive analytics goes one step further by using algorithms to recommend optimal actions ("what should I do") (Delen & Zolbanin, 2018, pp. 188–189). All analytics levels also reflect on the "why" behind (Delen & Demirkan, 2013, p. 361). In predictive and prescriptive analytics, AI is becoming increasingly important (Latinovic & Chatterjee, 2022, p. 968). AI "applies advanced analysis and logic-based techniques, including machine learning, to interpret events, support and automate decisions, and take actions" (Gartner, n. d.). Machine learning (ML) algorithms examine data, derive insights, and use what they have learned to inform decisions (Paschen et al., 2020, p. 405).

Despite its potential, advanced analytics is not yet systematically implemented in B2B marketing, and descriptive approaches often persist as they are easier to implement and less expensive (Fantini & Narayandas, 2023; Länsipuro & Karjaluoto, 2021, p. 22). According to Greiner et al. (2022, p. 98), companies should establish a foundation with descriptive analytics before leveraging predictive and prescriptive methods. Cogan & Orgis (2021, p. 220) argue that this also applies to lead management, where companies must first build a well-functioning process and ensure integrated systems and data flow before predictive analytics and AI can be integrated. Progressing through analytics levels increases the potential value, but also the complexity. Predictive and prescriptive methods require granular and high-quality data, stronger data literacy, and more advanced tools (Greiner et al., 2022, pp. 98–99).

Furthermore, in the context of lead management, it is helpful to distinguish between task automation and AI. The distinction is not always clear, as the goal of both concepts is to facilitate and improve human work (Zumstein et al., 2024, p. 18). Automation involves performing repetitive tasks based on predefined rules, but does not itself learn over time (Davenport et al., 2021, pp. 44–45). In contrast, AI models learn from data and make corresponding decisions (Rainsberger, 2022,

---

[1] Some authors further differentiate between descriptive and diagnostic analytics. Following Lepenioti et al. (2020, p. 57), this distinction is not made for the purposes of this thesis.

p. 11). A distinction is made between stand-alone and integrated automation or AI applications. CRM systems and marketing automation platforms might include AI functions to support lead scoring or deliver personalized content in lead nurturing, which is an example of integrated AI applications (Davenport et al., 2021, p. 46; Terstiege et al., 2021, p. 32). However, if rules need to be defined by marketers to conduct automated lead scoring or lead nurturing, this is an example of task automation (Gasser & Mäder, 2022, pp. 103–104; Järvinen & Taiminen, 2016, p. 165). Davenport (2021, p. 46) suggests that companies with little AI expertise should begin with task automation. As they accumulate experience and data, they can gradually move to ML techniques (Davenport et al., 2021, p. 46).

2.2.2 Prerequisites for Marketing Analytics Deployment

The effective deployment of marketing analytics depends on sound data management and the abilities and maturity of the technological infrastructure to support analytics (Delen & Demirkan, 2013, p. 361). Furthermore, organizational factors are crucial in enabling data-driven strategies (Wedel & Kannan, 2016, p. 97). In general, applying advanced analytics places more stringent requirements on companies (Vossebein et al., 2024, pp. 45–46).

Data Requirements

Although data management is not a focus of this thesis, it is helpful to provide a brief overview, since marketing analytics is based on information gathered about potential customers (Krieger, 2021, p. 155). When integrating analytics and automation, companies must ensure a clear overview of data sources and types (Zumstein et al., 2023, p. 62). B2B companies typically collect data from various sources to understand their potential customers' needs (Andersen et al., 2017, p. 2). Customer data is often stored in the CRM system. In addition, email marketing (e.g., click data), the website (e.g., form data), and digital analytics tools are important data sources (Zumstein et al., 2023, p. 62). Regarding data types, a distinction is made between demographic data (e.g., age group, position), company information (e.g., company size, industry),[2] and behavioral data (e.g., website visits, campaign responses) (Gasser & Mäder, 2022, p. 122). Behavioral data is particularly valuable for analytics and campaign targeting, as past actions

[2] Following D'Haen (2016, p. 69), the terms "company information" and "firmographic data" are used simultaneously in this thesis.

frequently indicate future behavior (Basu et al., 2023, p. 2590). It is usually gathered through digital analytics tools (Zumstein et al., 2023, p. 62).

In general, data quality, availability, accuracy, and completeness are essential for generating actionable insights and avoiding deceptive decision-making (Rosário & Dias, 2023, p. 11; Wedel & Kannan, 2016, p. 97). To enhance data quality and accuracy, the collected data must be processed. This includes cleansing, merging data from multiple sources, and managing data storage and access (Halfmann, 2022, p. 7). Advanced analytics needs a solid database to learn from in the first place. Therefore, to apply predictive analytics and AI in lead management, the availability of structured, granular lead data is a necessity. In practice, however, this is often not the case for companies (Vossebein et al., 2024, pp. 45–46).

Technological Requirements

In terms of technological requirements, data-driven marketing relies on technologies for collecting, processing, and analyzing data, while enabling process automation. A suitable combination of tools and technologies is crucial for effective analytics processes (Rosário & Dias, 2023, p. 8). The core systems described in Sect. 2.1.4, i.e., CRM systems and marketing automation, are essential in this regard. Their integrated analytics features provide a comprehensive overview of the customer journey by collecting and storing relevant data about potential customers (Rackley, 2015, pp. 105–106). While CRM systems remain central to data-driven marketing, digital analytics has broadened the scope and depth of customer data collection and analysis (Järvinen, 2016, p. 40). Järvinen (2016, p. 45) identifies web analytics, social media analytics, and marketing automation as essential applications for enhancing the understanding of interactions across digital touchpoints. These tools track the behavior of potential customers in the digital environment using cookies and IP addresses (Järvinen, 2016, p. 45). Marketing automation enables the identification of visitors and their long-term behavioral tracking (Sect. 2.3.3), while conventional web analytics is limited to monitoring aggregated visitor activity (Mero et al., 2020, p. 217). Social media analytics includes analytics in the realm of social media platforms such as LinkedIn and Facebook (Agnihotri et al., 2023, p. 110). Just as predictive analytics and AI place greater demands on data availability and quality, a higher level of technological maturity is required to apply advanced analytics. In lead management, such approaches should only be considered if systems and data sources are well-connected and integrated marketing automation is available (Cogan & Orgis, 2021, p. 220).

Organizational Requirements

Finally, the application of marketing data and analytics methods depends on the extent to which the corporate culture encourages data-driven decision-making (Wedel & Kannan, 2016, p. 97). Rosário & Dias (2023, p. 11) argue that this frequently requires significant organizational changes. An analytics-friendly corporate culture is characterized by employees who believe that understanding and applying various types of data is essential to the company's success (Kiron et al., 2013, p. 18). In this context, the involvement and support of the top management are crucial factors for successful data-driven processes (Länsipuro & Karjaluoto, 2021, p. 24). Additionally, marketing analytics requires access to personnel with technical and analytical expertise (Germann et al., 2013, p. 117). Companies should invest in developing these competencies internally through training and development programs (Andersen et al., 2017, pp. 6–7).

2.3 Improving B2B Lead Management with Marketing Analytics

Having outlined the fundamentals of B2B lead management and marketing analytics, this section focuses on combining these two concepts. It shows how data insights can be applied at different stages of the lead management process to inform decision-making and improve activities. The section concludes with the measurement of lead management effectiveness, which helps companies evaluate the impact of their efforts. Marketing analytics is applied across all stages of the marketing and sales funnel. Focus areas include target group and behavioral analysis and the evaluation of marketing success in customer acquisition (von Focht, 2022, p. 80).

Due to the identified research gap, this chapter is based on the conceptual transfer and combination of relevant research areas such as data-driven lead management, marketing analytics, customer journey analytics, and funnel performance management. This is achieved by examining specific applications that demonstrate how marketing analytics can improve lead generation, lead scoring, and lead nurturing, considering common challenges associated with each stage (Sect. 2.1.5). The section concludes with measuring effectiveness.

Figure 2.3 provides an overview of the topics covered in this section.

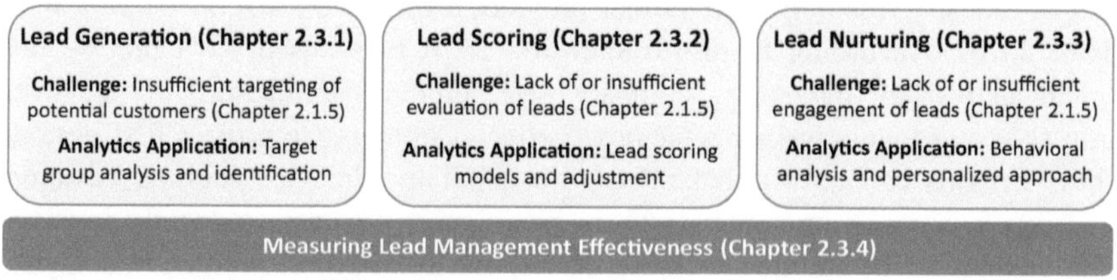

Fig. 2.3 Improving B2B Lead Management with Marketing Analytics. (Source: Own depiction)

The chapter is not exhaustive, and the expert interviews can further supplement or refine the discussed topics. Additionally, due to the limited adoption in practice, advanced analytics are described in the form of brief outlooks rather than explained in depth. An exception is predictive lead scoring, which the literature frequently discusses and directly contrasts with traditional models (e.g., González-Flores et al., 2025; Wu et al., 2024b). Lead handover is not considered separately, as it is naturally included in discussions about lead scoring and nurturing (e.g., Wenger, 2023). In addition, the coordination between marketing and sales is addressed within other chapters of this thesis.

2.3.1 Lead Generation: Optimizing Targeting

To ensure focused targeting, marketers must know the target group and its needs. Nevertheless, companies may encounter problems in addressing potential customers (Sect. 2.1.5). This section shows how marketing analytics can be used to overcome these issues.

According to Gebhardt & Gebhardt (2019, p. 77), the acquisition of new customers is based on clearly defined and segmented target groups. It is recommended to develop profiles of target customers, which can be informed by market research and customer interviews (Albrecht & Schlüter, 2022, p. 210; Vossebein et al., 2024, p. 22). In the B2B sector, developing an Ideal Customer Profile (ICP) and buyer personas are common approaches. The ICP describes the characteristics and attributes of companies that are best suited to a company's offerings and are most likely to become profitable and loyal customers. Buyer personas represent specific decision-makers within these ideal companies (Beck, 2025, p. 51; Honka & Durst, 2025, p. 32).

The industry research firm Gartner provides a framework for developing ICPs (Jain, 2024). According to this framework, an ICP is based on a precise historical analysis of data (e.g., company size, products purchased) on the most profitable and loyal customers or prospective customers from the CRM system. These insights can be supplemented with qualitative insights such as customer feedback surveys or interviews with internal teams who are frequently involved with customers. In addition to these descriptive approaches, predictive analytics can be used to analyze historical data and reveal patterns in lead behavior that could indicate future demands. The attributes considered in ICPs depend on the needs of the company, but can include firmographic data, the business situation, resources, or the business and operating model (Jain, 2024). ICPs serve as the foundation for targeting potentially valuable prospective customers through campaigns that are tailored to their specific needs and preferences (Beck, 2025, p. 51). Additionally, insights from ICPs can be considered when prioritizing and evaluating leads. Lastly, they serve as a starting point for developing buyer personas (Jain, 2024).

Since B2B transactions usually involve many stakeholders, it is essential to understand key decision-makers (Reklaitis & Pileliene, 2019, pp. 76–77). Buyer personas can provide an accurate picture of these individuals (N. Schuster, 2022, pp. 116–122) and represent the motivation behind the purchasing decision process (Körner, 2021, p. 67). Apart from demographic information, these semi-fictional profiles include behavioral data such as decision-making behavior, pain points, needs, and preferences of decision-makers (Honka & Durst, 2025, p. 32). In general, marketing and sales should develop buyer personas together. Apart from analyzing data of successful and loyal customers from the CRM system, a qualitative approach with surveys of existing or potential customers is also possible to determine what kind of information was or is relevant to the purchase decision (Dach, 2023, pp. 12–15; Körner, 2021, p. 69).

Overall, buyer personas enable a concrete determination of the content that is interesting for potential customers and offers them added value, as well as the channels that should be used to deliver the content (Körner, 2021, p. 69). Because they help marketers better understand and address their target audience, these profiles play an important role not only in lead generation but also in lead nurturing (Sect. 2.3.3) (N. Schuster, 2022, pp. 90–91).

Companies can also use AI-powered tools to create detailed persona profiles based on public data from websites and social media. One example is Delve AI, which uses various data sources such as CRM systems, Google Analytics, and social media to gain insights into the goals, needs, and values of buyer personas (Beck, 2025, pp. 53–54).

In practice, developing these profiles is a challenging task. It requires analyzing and combining different data sources and types of information (Jain, 2024). Nevertheless, these examples have demonstrated that knowledge of the ideal customer, as informed by marketing analytics, plays a crucial role in lead generation. It helps companies target the right potential customers from the start.

2.3.2 Lead Scoring: Evaluating and Prioritizing Leads

The literature acknowledges that recent advances in technology and analytics have significantly impacted lead qualification and scoring (D. Nair et al., 2020, p. 2). As mentioned in Sect. 2.1.5, companies frequently do not qualify their leads or do so insufficiently. This can result in poor lead quality presented to sales. According to Beco & Zeren (2023, p. 351), "one way out of such a predicament is to implement a lead scoring model [...] to ensure that leads are correctly qualified, developed, and handed over to sales at the right time." Therefore, this section focuses on lead scoring models in the broader context of lead qualification.

As indicated in Sect. 2.1.3, lead scoring allows companies to focus on leads with the highest suitability and strongest interest (Sharma et al., 2023, p. 262). By prioritizing high-quality leads, lead scoring can improve the productivity of sales teams and the effectiveness of outcomes through increased conversion rates (Wu et al., 2024b, p. 70). This, for example, affects the number of leads converted into Opportunities (Adobe, 2020, p. 47). According to Sharma et al. (2023, p. 262), lead scoring uses "data analytics to accurately assess the potential value of each lead." However, as described below, lead scoring models vary in their application of analytics. The literature often distinguishes between traditional and predictive models (González-Flores et al., 2025, p. 5; Wu et al., 2024b, p. 69). Since traditional models are based on rules derived from past events, they align with descriptive analytics (Sect. 2.2.1).

In practice, there are different options and criteria to build traditional lead scoring models (e.g., Adobe, 2020). Usually, leads are assigned scores based on explicit or implicit criteria or rules. Explicit variables are based on demographic and firmographic data (e.g., industry, number of employees, job title) to assess how well a lead aligns with the target group. Implicit attributes reflect behavioral data derived from the lead's engagement with touchpoints (e.g., number of website visits, email engagement, download of content) (Jadli et al., 2023, p. 1282; Wu et al., 2024b, p. 74). Different scores can be assigned depending on the profile fit and interaction, including negative values. For example, if a company wants to sell to large businesses, it could award 10 points for more than 1,000 employees and deduct 5 points for fewer than 50 employees. Additionally, 5 points could be awarded for downloading an e-book, and 20 points for downloading a product list (Gasser & Mäder, 2022, pp. 123–126). To develop powerful scoring models, companies should combine explicit and implicit criteria (González-Flores et al., 2025, pp. 5–6). As soon as a predefined score threshold is reached, the lead is processed by the sales team (Järvinen & Taiminen, 2016, p. 171). Due to the large number of leads generated in many companies, lead scoring should be automated via marketing automation (Wu et al., 2024b, p. 83). An advantage of lead scoring via such platforms is that analyses of the online behavior of leads can be conducted more easily (Beck, 2025, pp. 56–57). By reaching a predefined score, the lead is routed to sales automatically (Philipp, 2021, p. 231).

However, traditional lead scoring models exhibit disadvantages because the rules are set at the discretion of the marketer. This can lead to distortions and misconceptions (Gebhardt, 2023, p. 75). To counteract this issue, predictive lead scoring models have been studied in recent years (e.g., Jadli et al., 2023; Nygård & Mezei, 2020; Wu et al., 2024a). These models are based on ML to discern trends from historical data, extract features, and compute propensity scores. Models include classification, clustering, and regression. Consequently, predictive models are considered more effective and less biased than traditional models (Wu et al., 2024b, p. 77).

However, a recent study among B2B companies has shown that most companies focus on traditional methods, as only 2% of respondents indicated the use of AI-based lead scoring models (Zumstein et al., 2024, p. 41). This has been confirmed by Gebhardt & Gebhardt (2023, p. 76), who emphasize that point-based models prevail in practice. Reasons include a lack of capacity and know-how, poor data quality, complex implementation, and a lack of trust in advanced algorithms (Gebhardt, 2023, p. 75; Zumstein et al., 2024, p. 41). Issues can arise even with traditional lead scoring models when they are built on outdated datasets or based on poor data (Wu et al., 2024b, p. 84). As predictive lead scoring relies on high-quality data, it is questionable whether this approach is feasible for many companies, as discussed in Sect. 3.3.1.2.

In contrast to predictive lead scoring models that require minimal supervision, traditional lead scoring models must be continuously updated and adjusted after they have been introduced (Sharma et al., 2023, pp. 264–265). Marketing and sales should hold regular workshops to enable adaptations. They can, for example, conduct the following analyses (Adobe, 2020, p. 34; Huttelmaier & Heigl, 2023, pp. 311–312):

- Analysis of how many leads fall into a specific scoring category to identify problems with the lead scoring model (e.g., leads with negative or low scores).
- Evaluation of the disparities between rejected leads and those that evolved into Opportunities to adjust the criteria of the scoring model.
- Comparison of the explicit scores of leads that have recently become Opportunities with the scoring threshold to decide if the threshold needs to be adjusted.
- Testing different scoring models at the same time, which is possible in many marketing automation platforms, to determine which criteria are better suited.

The implementation of lead scoring models, the criteria used, and the adjustments required depend on the circumstances of the company and the availability of data (Gasser & Mäder, 2022, p. 130; González-Flores et al., 2025, p. 6).

This chapter has shown that lead scoring is crucial to identify and process high-quality leads. Marketing analytics can be used to develop traditional or predictive scoring models, although predictive models are still rarely implemented in practice. Additionally, data insights allow for the adaptation of lead scoring models. Lead nurturing, which often takes place in parallel with lead scoring, is discussed next.

2.3.3 Lead Nurturing: Enhancing Engagement

As described in Sect. 2.1.5, despite the importance of building relationships with potential customers, companies often fail to follow a consistent strategy. Thus, they cannot ensure a successful long-term engagement of leads. In this context, many companies still rely on standardized newsletters (Zumstein et al., 2024, pp. 14–15). This chapter discusses how marketing analytics can be used to counteract this issue. The focus is on marketing automation platforms, because they enable personalized lead nurturing (Järvinen & Taiminen, 2016, p. 165).

In general, lead nurturing is not limited to a single strategy. However, email marketing is considered important because it can be automated and personalized relatively easily (Gasser & Mäder, 2022, pp. 101–102). Apart from personalized email marketing, personal contact, for example, in the context of events, plays a crucial role (Zumstein et al., 2024, pp. 14–15). However, marketing automation has expanded the possibilities for lead nurturing. The literature often discusses the importance of marketing automation for behavioral tracking and delivering personalized content (e.g., Järvinen & Taiminen, 2016; Terho et al., 2022). After a lead has been generated and identified, marketing automation tracks the lead's behavior, which helps monitor how they engage with content over time. Based on this information and the stage in the customer journey, marketing can deliver targeted, relevant, and personalized content at the right time (Järvinen & Taiminen, 2016, pp. 170–173; Terho et al., 2022, pp. 300–302).

During the lead nurturing process, information is gathered not only by monitoring the behavior of a lead, but also through the contact information provided in forms and answers to questions (e.g., which topics they are interested in) (N. Schuster, 2021, p. 110). This process is an important feature of marketing automation, also known as progressive profiling. Based on the data that is collected about the lead, companies can enrich the individual lead profile. This also helps them adjust the general definition of buyer personas described in Sect. 2.3.1 (Körner, 2021, p. 72; Philipp, 2021, p. 206).

Based on the data that is gathered and processed about a lead, marketing automation initiates actions or processes based on preset triggers. In this context, marketers must set up clear guidelines for the automation, which corresponds to the principle of task automation (Sect. 2.2.1). Lead nurturing workflows are predefined processes that can be personalized based on a lead's actions. A specific activity, such as downloading a white paper, triggers the integration of the lead into a workflow that provides them with relevant content and topics (Gasser & Mäder, 2022, pp. 102–103). Therefore, the workflow follows an "if-then" principle. Depending on the position of the lead in the customer journey, different workflows can be relevant. For example, the lead's first action can trigger a welcome workflow with information about different offerings (N. Schuster, 2021, pp. 116–117). At a later stage, thematic workflows can be used to send suitable content based on the interests of the lead as identified through their online behavior. These workflows can result in more qualified contacts and increased conversion rates, as leads are developed according to their needs and interests (Gasser & Mäder, 2022, pp. 103–104).

In this context, marketing automation can be supported by AI. ML algorithms can analyze past customer behavior and predict future behavior. On this basis, workflows can be optimized or the timing of campaigns adjusted (Terstiege, 2022, p. 71). For example, according to a case study by Cogan & Orgis (2021, p. 209), the implementation of the tool Motiva-AI, an AI-based extension of the marketing automation platform Oracle Eloqua, has contributed to higher email open rates and increased conversion rates at the case company. The tool was used to implement an independent and automatic optimization of campaigns. This included automatic adjustment of the frequency and timing of emails based on data analysis (Cogan & Orgis, 2021, p. 209).

As indicated, personalization is an important concept in lead nurturing and is considered a fundamental advantage of data-driven marketing. Based on the data collected about potential customers, personalized campaigns can be developed that can contribute to increased conversion rates (Rosário & Dias, 2023, p. 10). This is crucial in B2B markets, because the smaller number of customers compared to B2C requires businesses to create and maintain meaningful relationships (Hallikainen et al., 2020, p. 91). In lead nurturing, personalization should go beyond mentioning the name of the lead in a newsletter. Instead, the content itself should be tailored to the lead's interests (Järvinen & Taiminen, 2016, p. 165; Terstiege, 2022, p. 72).

In the context of personalization, the literature also occasionally discusses the potential of AI. If included in marketing automation, AI may assist in automatically determining customer interests, continuously identifying patterns, and forecasting future channel usage. This is associated with higher conversion rates, as content can be presented in an even more targeted and personalized way (Terstiege, 2022, pp. 72–73). Another promising avenue to nurture leads through AI is that it can record user behavior and display personalized content on a company's website. In this way, "AI […] becomes a content curator that provides each individual lead with tailor-made content" (Hilgenstock & Kuhle, 2022, p. 57).

This chapter has highlighted the importance of marketing analytics in nurturing leads through behavioral analysis and a personalized approach. This can be achieved by leveraging marketing automation. Although processes are traditionally rule-based, there is an increasing possibility of AI support. After presenting applications of marketing analytics in the various stages of the lead management process, the next chapter focuses on measuring lead management effectiveness, which was identified as another dimension of marketing analytics in the introduction.

2.3.4 Measuring Lead Management Effectiveness

Accurate measurement in lead management allows marketing to adjust approaches and improve future outcomes (Stevens, 2012, pp. 9–10). In this context, Andersen et al. (2017, p. 7) emphasize the importance of "a comprehensive end-to-end measurement capability with proper attribution throughout the buying journey." However, in the B2B sector, performance measurement is complicated by several factors. These include long and complex sales cycles that involve multiple parties and a lack of information on the development of leads after handover to the sales team (Stevens, 2012, p. 176). Therefore, in addition to relevant metrics, this section discusses options for funnel performance management and sales feedback.

Relevant Metrics

According to Rackley (2015, pp. 2–3), measuring marketing performance involves several steps: determining which metrics are most relevant, measuring how well they contribute to achieving predetermined objectives over time, and leveraging the findings to improve marketing performance. In lead management, the selection of metrics depends on the company's circumstances (Vossebein et al., 2024, p. 42). Therefore, a list of possible metrics is not provided at this point. Nevertheless, some authors (e.g., Beco & Zeren, 2023, pp. 351–353) offer detailed overviews of potential indicators and metrics across the stages of the marketing and sales funnel. Huttelmaier & Heigl (2023, p. 308) emphasize that "it is important to not overcomplicate lead management controlling." This is especially true for companies with low data usage (Länsipuro & Karjaluoto, 2021, pp. 28–29). Relevant key figures should be defined jointly by marketing and sales and collected and analyzed regularly (Beco & Zeren, 2023, p. 357).

As described in the introduction, the success of lead management can be measured from the perspective of effectiveness or efficiency. Efficiency refers to the utilization of resources per lead (Wenger, 2023, pp. 493–494), often measured as the cost per lead or, ultimately, the cost of converting and acquiring a new customer (Dach, 2023, p. 39). As mentioned, the focus of this thesis is on improvements regarding effectiveness. Therefore, following Wenger (2023, p. 93), this chapter discusses effectiveness as reflected in the quantity of leads, lead quality, and conversion rates. More qualified leads improve conversion rates (Mattos et al., 2021, p. 91), and improving conversion rates decreases the cost of acquiring customers (Espadinha-Cruz et al., 2021, p. 3). In addition, companies should consider the revenue generated, as not all conversions are of equal economic value (Gasser & Mäder, 2022, p. 53).

Regarding lead quantity, it can be measured how many new leads were generated by channel and campaign (Beco & Zeren, 2023, p. 351; Rackley, 2015, p. 69). The number of MQLs that marketing passes on to sales is another important quantitative metric. Unintentionally decreasing numbers can indicate ineffective lead generation and nurturing. This means, for example, campaigns or content fail to reach the intended audience, or inadequate channels are used (Huttelmaier & Heigl, 2023, p. 308). However, an exclusive focus on quantity can result in the handover of many low-quality MQLs. Sales might not pursue these leads, resulting in a waste of resources (Wenger, 2023, pp. 500–501; Woelke,

2021, p. 216). Therefore, Huttelmaier & Heigl (2023, p. 299) emphasize that it is important to "find the optimal balance between quantity and quality of leads passed on from marketing to sales to maximize sales conversions".

Conversion rates are considered a central metric for measuring marketing effectiveness (Neumüller & Bigliel, 2023, p. 242). According to Gasser & Mäder (2022, pp. 50–51), "the conversion rate is the proportion of target persons whose status has changed, e.g., from a prospect to a customer, from an MQL to an SQL, etc., along the entire customer journey." Therefore, conversion rates can be calculated and analyzed along all lead qualification levels (Dach, 2023, p. 40; Gasser & Mäder, 2022, p. 53). The MQL-SAL[3] conversion rate is an important metric that represents the ratio of marketing-qualified leads to leads accepted by sales. When the ratio is near 1 or 100%, it means that higher-quality leads are passed on to sales. In contrast, a lower rate indicates that less qualified and promising leads are handed over (Huttelmaier & Heigl, 2023, p. 308; Wenger, 2023, p. 501). This ratio also demonstrates how closely marketing and sales are aligned in lead management (Andersen et al., 2018, p. 5). To evaluate activities in lead generation and nurturing, another important quality metric for marketing is how many and which MQLs converted into customers (Huttelmaier & Heigl, 2023, p. 308).

Lead quality should be assessed in relation to individual campaigns, channels, and content types. This way, marketing can evaluate which campaigns are most effective and which content and channels contribute to a faster progression or better conversion. Based on this, they can adjust future marketing activities (Huttelmaier & Heigl, 2023, pp. 308–309). In this context, companies must continuously analyze and test different strategies to prioritize the most effective and cost-efficient approaches (Świeczak & Łukowski, 2016, pp. 127–129).

Most of the metrics described in this chapter are available in marketing automation and CRM systems. Depending on individual needs, they can be reported on a daily, weekly, monthly, or quarterly basis (Beco & Zeren, 2023, p. 353). The outcomes are visualized in dashboards that compare the current performance with the previously defined objectives. These dashboards can be accessed through CRM systems, marketing automation platforms, or Business Intelligence (BI) tools (Klaus, 2023, pp. 447–448). In addition to conversion rates, the number of leads, and the revenue generated, dashboards can also provide information on individual campaign and channel performance (Klaus, 2023, p. 448). Vossebein et al. (2024, p. 41) emphasize that dashboards should be easy

[3] Depending on the company's definitions, this can also refer to the MQL-SQL rate (Andersen et al., 2018, p. 5).

to understand so that employees can derive insights quickly. According to Klaus (2023, p. 448), "impactful dashboards are not only used for reporting purposes, but also for operational steering." This is essential to derive findings and take action (Klaus, 2023, p. 448). After introducing important metrics, the following chapter deals with funnel performance management, a method for tracking leads along the marketing and sales funnel.

Funnel Performance Management

Andersen et al. (2018, p. 4) point out that many companies do not track outcomes within the marketing and sales funnel. As a result, marketing cannot understand which measures are effective and whether leads have become customers. That is why continuous tracking of leads per stage along the marketing and sales funnel is crucial (Andersen et al., 2018, p. 5). This requires common goals, joint definitions between marketing and sales, and feedback processes regarding the quality of marketing-generated leads (Huttelmaier & Heigl, 2023, p. 308).

Instead of considering metrics individually, Beco & Zeren (2023, pp. 347–360) advocate for funnel performance management. This can help track lead behavior, identify bottlenecks, and derive potential for improvement (Beco & Zeren, 2023, pp. 354–355). The authors define several prerequisites: a jointly defined funnel that is managed by the marketing and sales departments, lead scoring that is continuously refined and adapted to the company, and metrics that are consistently measured. This, for example, refers to conversion rates that should be monitored across the stages of lead development (Beco & Zeren, 2023, p. 355). As shown in Fig. 2.4, the funnel is divided into top, middle, and bottom of funnel. The outcome of the funnel is revenue, which, according to Rackley (2015, p. 34), is "the end game for marketing analytics."

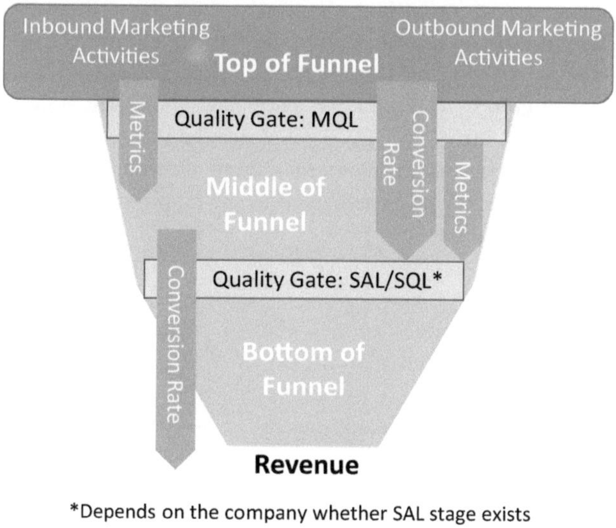

Fig. 2.4 Funnel Performance Management. (Source: Adapted from Beco & Zeren (2023, p. 356)[4])

Neumüller & Bigliel (2023, pp. 241–242) point out that many B2B companies concentrate on leads that have been successfully converted and on increasing conversion rates. However, they often ignore insights from leads who drop out of the funnel before making a purchase. According to the authors, companies can improve their marketing strategies and recover the value of otherwise wasted marketing resources in lead generation and lead qualification by understanding the reasons for these abandonments (Neumüller & Bigliel, 2023, pp. 243–244).

Finally, feedback from sales regarding lead quality is considered crucial in measuring lead management performance (Andersen et al., 2018, p. 5). It is recommended that marketing receive feedback on every lead forwarded. Apart from determining whether the individual lead was rejected or accepted, marketing must understand the reasons behind the decision of sales to improve lead generation and scoring. Huttelmaier & Heigl (2023, pp. 310–311) recommend that this

---

[4] The depiction of lead qualification levels is deliberately simplified. Additional stages (e.g., Opportunities) are omitted for clarity.

should include an evaluation of both the lead's target group fit and whether they were ready for sales, i.e., ready to buy. Marketing should provide a simple form that allows sales to quickly provide feedback on lead quality (e.g., "bad fit" in terms of the target group). This could be automated via the CRM system or email (Huttelmaier & Heigl, 2023, pp. 309–310). After the theoretical part has laid the foundations for B2B lead management, marketing analytics, and the combination of both concepts, the next part is dedicated to the empirical findings.

Research Approach and Empirical Findings

3

After the theoretical framework has been established in the previous chapter, this section presents the research methodology and the empirical insights from the expert interviews.

3.1 Methodology

The approach for data collection is described first, followed by the evaluation method.

3.1.1 Data Collection Using Expert Interviews

A qualitative research approach was chosen because this research is not concerned with quantitative representativeness but rather with gaining a deep understanding of the various aspects of the research problem (Almeida et al., 2017, p. 370). One possibility to collect qualitative data is through expert interviews, which are usually conducted as semi-structured interviews (Helfferich, 2022, pp. 887–888). These interviews follow a previously developed guideline that provides a clear structure for the conversation and allows the researcher to guide and steer the data collection process (Bogner et al., 2014, pp. 27–28; Misoch, 2019, pp. 66–67).

Supplementary Information The online version contains supplementary material available at https://doi.org/10.1007/978-3-658-50959-0_3

L. Hannemann, *Integrating Marketing Analytics Approaches into B2B Lead Management*, BestMasters, https://doi.org/10.1007/978-3-658-50959-0_3

Expert interviews are primarily defined by the group of individuals being interviewed (Helfferich, 2022, p. 875). According to Przyborski & Wohlrab-Sahr (2021, p. 157), experts "have specific role knowledge, are ascribed such knowledge and claim a special competence based on this for themselves." Expert interviews try to capture practical and experience-related knowledge in a specific field (Helfferich, 2022, p. 888). They are the method of choice for this thesis for several reasons. Firstly, as Przyborski & Wohlrab-Sahr (2021, p. 163) argue, expert interviews are valuable to understand a phenomenon that is not well-documented. Due to the identified research gap, the research question cannot be answered by only reviewing the literature. The thesis aims to address the issue through additional insights from business practice. Expert interviews are also well-suited to generate insights into organizational processes (Bogner et al., 2014, pp. 18–19). Lastly, they aim to provide a deeper analysis of a small number of individual cases instead of covering as many cases as possible (R. Kaiser, 2021, p. 7). This offers insights into use cases and best practices for the practical guide.

In this study, a purposive sample was used, which means that the researcher intentionally selects individuals who are expected to contribute particularly well to answering the research question (Farrugia, 2019, p. 70). The experts were selected based on their position and functional knowledge in marketing-related B2B lead management. All experts worked in B2B companies and represent a homogeneous sample (Farrugia, 2019, p. 70). However, attention was paid to cover different industries. One interviewee represented a B2B marketing agency to provide an external viewpoint. The sample size was twelve, which, according to Baker & Edwards (2012, p. 10), is appropriate for a master's thesis. Potential interviewees received a contact letter (Appendix 2 in the Electronic Supplementary Material) that included assurances of anonymity and a note regarding the audio recording (von dem Berge, 2020, p. 285). Most experts requested the interview guide in advance. The researcher concluded that, given the specific nature of the topic, the experts wanted to familiarize themselves with the content beforehand (Bogner et al., 2014, pp. 30–31). Table 3.1 provides an overview of the interviews.

Table 3.1 Key Features of the Expert Interviews

Expert	Expert's Role	Company	Company Industry	Company Size	Interview Duration
E1	Team Lead Digital Marketing	C1	Wholesale	Large	30:45 min
E2a, E2b	Director Growth Marketing, Growth Marketing Specialist	C2	Technology	Large	32:01 min
E3	Online Marketing Specialist	C3	IT Services and Consulting	Large	33:17 min
E4	Owner and Managing Director	C4	Digital Marketing Agency	Small	44:19 min
E5	Marketing Manager Marketing Automation and Lead Management	C5	Manufacturing	Large	37:16 min
E6	Head of Corporate Marketing and Communications	C6	Manufacturing	Large	28:55 min
E7	Marketing Director	C7	Technology	Large	33:08 min
E8	Direct Marketing Specialist	C8	IT Services and Consulting	Large	29:21 min
E9	Marketing Specialist	C9	Manufacturing	Medium-sized	22:21 min
E10	Head of Marketing	C10	Manufacturing	Large	32:23 min
E11	Team Lead Marketing	C11	IT Services and Consulting	Medium-sized	31:30 min
E12	Head of Marketing	C12	Manufacturing	Large	28:47 min

Source: Own depiction

For anonymization purposes, the experts were pseudonymized with designations such as "E1." Moreover, designations such as "C1" were used for the companies. The experts' roles cover a broad spectrum of B2B lead management and represent a range of industries and company sizes. In highly generalized terms, the industries include wholesale, technology, IT services and consulting, manufacturing, and a digital marketing agency. Most companies are classified as large enterprises.[1] The interviews were conducted in May and June 2025 via Microsoft Teams over a period of four weeks. Depending on the mother tongue of the expert, the interviews were held in German or English. At the beginning of each interview, explicit verbal consent was obtained for the recording (Agarwal, 2019, pp. 83–85).

The research question serves as the starting point for data collection and the development of the interview guide (Mayer, 2012, p. 45). Kaiser (2021, p. 68) emphasizes the importance of operationalization, which involves a step-by-step translation of the research problem into guiding interview questions. This ensures that the collected data can be linked back to the research question (R. Kaiser, 2021, p. 69). The operationalization of the interview questions is presented in Appendix 3 in the Electronic Supplementary Material, and the final interview guide is available in Appendix 4 in the Electronic Supplementary Material. A set of main questions was developed, and optional follow-up questions were prepared and used during the interviews if not answered through the main questions (Bogner et al., 2014, pp. 28–29; Przyborski & Wohlrab-Sahr, 2021, pp. 160–161). Depending on the expert's area of responsibility, the questions were asked in a slightly modified form. In addition, a customized version was created for the marketing agency expert (Bogner et al., 2014, p. 30).

The interview recordings are transcribed by converting audio sequences into written text (Bogner et al., 2014, p. 41). The research goals determine the design of the transcription system (Wollin-Giering et al., 2024, pp. 4–5). This thesis used the transcription rules by Dresing & Pehl (2018, pp. 21–22). They were modified to reflect the research interest, which prioritizes content over linguistic peculiarities. Therefore, the spoken word was adapted to written standards by eliminating unnecessary repetitions and grammatical errors (Bucholtz, 2000, p. 1461; McMullin, 2023, p. 141). The final transcription rules are listed in Appendix 5 in the Electronic Supplementary Material.

---

[1] Official categories based on the number of employees: Small companies (10–49 employees), medium-sized companies (50–249 employees), and large companies (more than 250 employees) (Eurostat, n. d.). The actual employee numbers within these categories varied significantly among the interviewed companies.

3.1.2 Data Evaluation Through Qualitative Content Analysis

The transcription is followed by data evaluation, which, in qualitative studies, is often conducted using qualitative content analysis (Stamann et al., 2016, p. 1). Schreier (2014) provides an overview of different versions of this analysis method. This thesis uses the content-structuring approach, a frequently used variant that enables structured processing of the collected material (Schreier, 2014, pp. 5–6). The approach proposed by Kuckartz & Rädiker (2024, pp. 129–132) was chosen because it combines deductive and inductive category formation. This is relevant for the present research because it allows a flexible approach that combines theory and practice. In the following, the analysis steps according to Kuckartz & Rädiker's model are explained and directly applied to the research.

The first step is the initial text work, during which the researcher highlights important passages and writes memos to record first ideas (Kuckartz & Rädiker, 2024, pp. 132–133). It is also helpful to build case summaries to identify similarities and differences between interviews (Kuckartz & Rädiker, 2024, pp. 124–128). The essence of content-structuring approaches is the development of categories that are grouped in a system and applied to the material (Schreier, 2014, p. 5). Categories can be formed deductively, i.e., derived from the theoretical reference in advance, or inductively, i.e., developed from the collected material (Linneberg & Korsgaard, 2019, pp. 263–264). Kuckartz & Rädiker's approach combines both methods, where the categories represent topics and subtopics of the study. The main categories are usually defined deductively and can be taken directly from the interview guide (Kuckartz & Rädiker, 2024, p. 133). The text passages are first coded with the main categories, compiled, and then coded again with inductively developed subcategories. The category system is continuously reviewed, adjusted, and refined (Kuckartz & Rädiker, 2024, pp. 134–142). The next step is to analyze and interpret the identified themes. Depending on the research, these may include category-based analyses or in-depth case analyses. The final step is presenting the results of the evaluation process (Kuckartz & Rädiker, 2024, pp. 147–154).

Despite the availability of translated interview transcripts, the qualitative content analysis was carried out using the original transcripts to preserve the meaning. The program MAXQDA 2024 was used to facilitate the evaluation process (MAXQDA, n. d.). As part of the initial text work, case summaries were created. Those served as a rough classification of the interviews and facilitated the formation of categories. The main categories served as guiding principles during data collection in the form of dimensions of analysis and question complexes (Appendix 3 in the Electronic Supplementary Material) and could be directly derived from the interview guide. After four interviews had been coded, the category system could be differentiated into concrete subcategories. Therefore, separate coding using the main categories was no longer necessary. The main categories *lead management maturity* and *extent of data-driven decision-making* were exceptions. Appendix 6 in the Electronic Supplementary Material provides an overview of the final categories. Only text passages that contributed to answering the research questions were coded. The final category system, including definitions and delimitations, is available in Appendix 7 in the Electronic Supplementary Material. To protect the anonymity and confidentiality of the participating experts and companies, the corresponding anchor examples as well as the original interview transcripts are not disclosed in this publication.

Once all coded segments were compiled, the categories or subcategories were evaluated. The first step was to understand the status quo of lead management from a marketing perspective within the interviewed companies. This was followed by an analysis of marketing analytics in lead management. The analysis concluded with the success factors for integrating marketing analytics into B2B lead management. Considering the empirical framework, the empirical section presents insights gained from the expert interviews. As the results are based on qualitative data, they are not exhaustive but focus on recurring themes and individual use cases.

3.2 Lead Management Processes in B2B Companies

To answer the research question, lead management processes in the interviewed companies needed to be examined first. This included the maturity level, the technological infrastructure, and challenges and bottlenecks. Although not a conscious goal, there were significant differences between the companies in terms of maturity and technological infrastructure.

3.2.1 Lead Management Maturity

This chapter provides a broad overview of the maturity of lead management processes coded under the category *lead management maturity*. The companies were categorized based on Wenger's maturity model from a marketing-oriented perspective. As the marketing-sales relationship was less tangible, this dimension was examined throughout the rest of the empirical section and not interpreted at this point. As Fig. 3.1 shows, the companies exhibited different degrees of maturity. This ranged from the first implementation of a marketing-oriented lead management process to fully standardized processes. A detailed overview of the process stages per interviewed company is provided in Appendix 8 in the Electronic Supplementary Material.

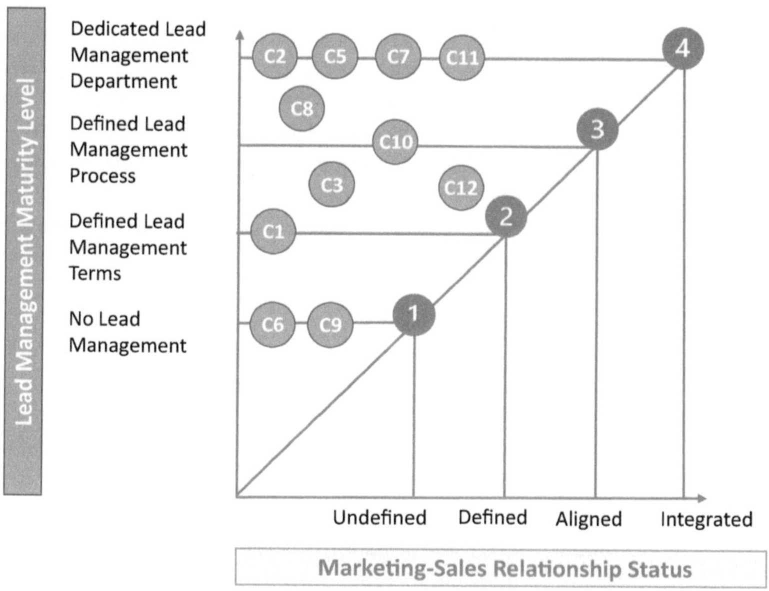

Fig. 3.1 Lead Management Maturity in Interviewed Companies. (Source: Own depiction based on the concept of Wenger (2023, p. 502)[2] and the expert interviews)

No Lead Management from a Marketing Perspective

At C6 and C9, marketing was not yet involved in the lead management process. This means that lead management, including lead generation, had been carried out exclusively by the sales team. From a marketing perspective, this corresponds to

[2] The categorization is based on the criteria for Wenger's maturity model (Sect. 2.1.1) but required interpretation by the researcher. Some companies were placed between maturity levels if they met additional criteria. C4 has been omitted from the model as it represents the perspective of an external agency.

the lowest stage in Wenger's maturity model. However, in addition to the existing sales processes, both companies planned to link lead management to marketing in the future (E6, 2025, pos. 2; E9, 2025, pos. 5).

Defined Lead Management Terms from a Marketing Perspective

In other companies, marketing was responsible for lead generation only. C1 forwarded leads generated via its website directly to sales without qualification or prioritization. Due to the lack of a CRM system, this corresponds to the second-lowest maturity level (E1, 2025, pos. 3–7; 14). Similarly, at C3, contacts were identified after completing a form, added to the CRM system, and directly handed over. Software support and rough lead qualification levels were in place, which is why C3 was placed slightly above the second level (E3, 2025, pos. 5–10; 38).

At C12, marketing conducted an initial qualification before handing over the generated leads. This was done manually and without lead qualification levels (E12, 2025, pos. 3–5; 21). Since software support was available, the placement was slightly above the second level.

Defined Lead Management Process from a Marketing Perspective

At C10, marketing leads were generated through different digital and offline channels. They were transferred to the CRM system, manually enriched with information, and qualified in clear stages (E10, 2025, pos. 5–10; 32). This corresponds to the third level of Wenger's model. At C8, following lead generation and initial qualification, manual lead scoring was used to prioritize leads before passing them to sales. Due to distinct lead qualification levels and clear responsibilities, C8 was placed slightly above maturity level three (E8, 2025, pos. 3–5; 37).

Dedicated Lead Management Department (Team) from a Marketing Perspective

At three companies, marketing was involved in all stages of the standardized and clearly defined lead management process (E2, 2025, pos. 5–6; E5, 2025, pos. 3–5; E7, 2025, pos. 7–9). The processes at C2 and C7 were similar, which is likely because both operate in the technology industry. After leads were collected primarily through the website and events, they were transferred to the marketing automation system, where missing data was added, and lead scoring was applied. This triggered an automation that transferred the leads to the CRM system, from where they were routed to sales (E2, 2025, pos. 4; E7, 2025, pos. 5; 17). At C5, generated leads were evaluated according to their buying intent. Based on this, they could be forwarded directly to sales or go through lead scoring and lead nurturing by passing through different automated lead nurturing workflows in the marketing automation system (E5, 2025, pos. 7–11).

At these companies, there were indications that a separate team within marketing was responsible for lead management (E2, 2025, pos. 15; E5, 2025, pos. 3; E7, 2025, pos. 33). In addition, they employed clear terminology and dedicated software support with a high degree of automation. Therefore, these companies appeared to have the most mature lead management practices, corresponding to the highest maturity level in Wenger's model. At C11, a separate lead management department served as a link between marketing and sales, which was responsible for lead qualification and handover (E11, 2025, pos. 2–4). The marketing department engaged in lead generation and nurturing using automated workflows (E11, 2025, pos. 12–14).

The assessment of this category revealed different lead management maturity levels. This also included the scope of marketing involvement and the degree of automation. The agency expert confirmed this finding, observing a range of maturity levels in practice (E4, 2025, pos. 5–6). As described in the following chapters, these differences formed the basis for understanding the technological infrastructure and challenges that the companies faced.

3.2.2 Technological Infrastructure for Lead Management and Analytics

The technological infrastructure was considered in a separate category, as software support is only considered marginally in Wenger's model. However, the technological infrastructure and the degree of automation were recurring issues throughout the interviews. This chapter presents an overview of the systems and tools at a high level, along with their basic functions as described by the experts. Concrete applications will be explored in later chapters. Two deductive subcategories, *core systems*, i.e., CRM systems and marketing automation platforms (Sect. 2.1.4), and *further analytics tools*, were formed. The further analytics tools considered web analytics or social media analytics tools (Sect. 2.2.2).

Of all interviews, C1 stood out because it did not use a CRM system. This resulted in a high level of manual effort with Excel lists and made it difficult to access data when setting up marketing activities (E1, 2025, pos. 13–15). All remaining companies had a CRM system as part of their core infrastructure for lead management or planned to use it as part of the marketing-oriented lead management process in the future. Three companies used Microsoft Dynamics 365, and Salesforce was mentioned twice. C10 was looking for a new CRM system at the time of the interview and also considered these two providers (E10, 2025, pos. 28–30). Other experts mentioned SAP Sales Cloud (E6, 2025, pos. 2) and SAP C4C (E8, 2025, pos. 11).

Even though some scholars highlight the increased importance of marketing automation in the DACH region (Sect. 2.1.4), only four companies actively utilized it in lead management. These were the companies with the highest lead management maturity. Vendors included Oracle Eloqua, Salesforce Pardot, and Click, which is an add-on for Microsoft Dynamics (Click, 2024; E11, 2025, pos. 9–10). Two of the companies that used marketing automation extensively were American companies, and another expert worked for a European company in the US. However, their lead management processes were globally standardized, or implemented with slight adaptations (E2, 2025, pos. 13; E5, 2025, pos. 5; E7, 2025, pos. 7–9). Therefore, it can be assumed that marketing automation strategies were also used in other markets. Other experts stated that subsidiaries of their companies abroad, especially in the US or China, already relied more on marketing automation (E8, 2025, pos. 31; E10, 2025, pos. 14).

The comparatively lower adoption of marketing automation tools in German companies could be because of stricter data protection regulations in Europe. These regulations affect the collection and tracking of personal data and require a careful selection of tools (Lammenett, 2024, pp. 642–643). However, platforms such as HubSpot or Salesforce can be used in a GDPR-friendly manner if the corresponding functions are applied actively and correctly (HubSpot, n. d.-b; Radchenko, 2024). Other reasons for the lower adoption in some companies could be missing resources or know-how (Zumstein et al., 2023, p. 25). One expert stated that the reason was the lack of a marketing automation function within their current CRM system and thus a technical limitation (E10, 2025, pos. 4). Nevertheless, multiple experts emphasized that they planned the use of marketing automation (E6, 2025, pos. 4; E8, 2025, pos. 31; E10, 2025, pos. 36). At two other companies, the CRM system included a marketing automation function which was not yet used for lead scoring or nurturing (E3, 2025, pos. 12; E12, 2025, pos. 9).

Overall, this subcategory has shown that although marketing automation is highlighted in the literature as an important part of the technological infrastructure for lead management, most interviewed companies did not yet use it or not to its full potential. However, almost all experts used a CRM system, often as an enterprise platform. These differences impact the ability to apply marketing analytics, as Sect. 3.3 will show.

Regarding further analytics tools, several experts mentioned web analytics. A specific tool was Google Analytics, or as per the new version, Google Analytics 4

(Google Analytics, n. d.), which was used for monitoring website behavior "further up the funnel" (E5, 2025, pos. 11). One expert mentioned that the company switched to the tool Matomo, which they considered more GDPR-compliant (E3, 2025, pos. 43–44). Another expert referred to social media analytics, for example, for Facebook or LinkedIn (E5, 2025, pos. 11). In addition, some experts highlighted BI tools. Because they serve the purpose of reporting, they are discussed in more detail in Sect. 3.3.2.3. Table 3.2 summarizes the technological infrastructure, and Appendix 8 in the Electronic Supplementary Material embeds it into the processes as described by the experts.

Table 3.2 Technological Infrastructure for Lead Management and Analytics

Subcategory	Applications	Tool Examples	Main Functions Mentioned
Core Systems	CRM Systems	Salesforce, Microsoft Dynamics 365, HubSpot, SAP Sales Cloud, SAP C4C	Central Database for Lead Records, Lead Creation and Qualification, Data Enrichment, Lead Status Tracking, Reporting
	Marketing Automation Platforms	Oracle Eloqua, Salesforce Pardot, Click, HubSpot, SAP Marketing Cloud	Lead Capture, Lead Scoring, Lead Nurturing, Lead Routing, Campaign Execution
Further Analytics Tools	Web Analytics	Google Analytics / Google Analytics 4, Matomo	Website Behavior Monitoring, Web Optimization
	Social Media Analytics	No mention of tools	Reports from Individual Social Media Platforms

Source: Own depiction based on the expert interviews[3]

After laying the groundwork, the next section deals with challenges and bottlenecks in lead management. Here, the differences between companies in terms of process maturity and the technological infrastructure became increasingly evident.

[3] The overview reflects interviewee responses and is therefore not exhaustive.

3.2.3 Challenges and Bottlenecks in Lead Management

The challenges presented in Sect. 2.1.5 were the starting point for building subcategories. These dimensions were further refined and supplemented through inductive analysis. The subcategories representing the process and people dimension were *process definition issues and marketing-sales misalignment* and *issues at lead management process stages.* The data and technology dimension included *data gaps and quality issues* and *technological limitations.*

Process Definition Issues and Marketing-Sales Misalignment

Experts frequently mentioned problems related to the definition of the lead management process and the cooperation between departments, especially between marketing and sales. E4 (2025, pos. 12) described a "lack of clarity about what should be achieved [...]" among many B2B clients. This was accompanied by missing definitions or different interpretations of a lead and what constitutes a good lead (E3, 2025, pos. 16; E6, 2025, pos. 30). Consequently, departments often pursued different goals in lead management (E4, 2025, pos. 12). These fundamental problems in process definition and clarity were highlighted mainly by experts whose companies had been assigned a lower lead management maturity level.

Several experts considered coordination with sales to be a challenge. As one expert put it, "we lack insight once the lead is handed over" (E2, 2025, pos. 12). Another interviewee agreed that "although we from marketing communicate a lot to sales, communication in the other direction often does not take place" (E11, 2025, pos. 12). For C11, this led to marketing not knowing how the leads developed and whether they turned into customers. Although this information was available to marketing at C2, they lacked insight into the reason why a lead was rejected by sales (E2, 2025, pos. 12). In this context, the importance of feedback loops described in Sect. 2.3.4 becomes evident. Experts also noted the insufficient follow-up of marketing-generated leads, which is described as the "sales lead black hole." This was attributed to a lack of capacity (E5, 2025, pos. 13) and inadequate incentive systems (E2, 2025, pos. 31; E10, 2025, pos. 16). These problems were mentioned by companies with largely automated processes, which indicates that technological maturity cannot compensate for alignment issues.

Issues at Lead Management Process Stages

The experts also mentioned issues at individual stages of the lead management process. These challenges were separated from the subcategory presented above because they form the basis for the marketing analytics applications in Sect. 3.3.1.

Even though problems related to lead generation were less frequently mentioned, some companies faced challenges in approaching the right contacts in their target group (E12, 2025, pos. 13) or reaching their target group at all (E9, 2025, pos. 11). According to the agency expert, some B2B clients were unsure about "who should be reached" (E4, 2025, pos. 12). In addition, not all companies could assess which tactics and channels were most effective in generating leads (E9, 2025, pos. 17) or only recently began collecting and evaluating relevant data (E11, 2025, pos. 20; E12, 2025, pos. 23).

Some companies lacked thorough lead qualification in marketing, which resulted in unsatisfactory prequalification for sales. The evaluation of leads was limited to ad hoc assessments of individual measures (E3, 2025, pos. 38) or manual research without qualification levels (E12, 2025, pos. 21). One expert summarized their approach as follows: "It's simply like, they could be interesting, then they go to sales. Or, probably not, and then they are ignored" (E12, 2025, pos. 21). This aligns with earlier findings about a lack of lead qualification or the reliance on simple criteria, resulting in intuitive decisions (Sect. 2.1.5). Only four out of twelve experts reported using lead scoring. Consequently, for others, it was difficult to assess the value of leads and prioritize the most promising ones for sales (E3, 2025, pos. 34; E12, 2025, pos. 25).

Similarly, experts reported a lack of or insufficient use of lead nurturing, especially in an automated and consistent way. Leads were often quickly handed over to sales, which prevented further engagement and qualification in marketing (E1, 2025, pos. 7; E3, 2025, pos. 22). Other experts described challenges in the development of leads toward sales readiness, because they lacked a consistent nurturing strategy (E10, 2025, pos. 54; E12, 2025, pos. 9). Consequently, they were not able to pass on leads to sales "with a clear conscience" (E10, 2025, pos. 36). These issues confirm previous findings in the literature (Sect. 2.1.5).

Overall, problems in this subcategory were particularly mentioned by companies with a lower maturity level in lead management. Companies with a higher maturity level had already implemented and developed process stages further, as later chapters will show.

Data Gaps and Quality Issues

In line with the literature, several experts discussed poor data quality and inconsistent data collection. This included incorrect or incomplete contact details (E2, 2025, pos. 13). The inadequate maintenance of CRM systems caused the systems to contain unassigned or incomplete contacts, which made it challenging to target specific industries and resulted in unreliable databases (E4, 2025, pos. 17–18; E12, 2025, pos. 19). Two experts noted the lack of data maintenance by sales as a further reason for gaps in data quality (E1, 2025, pos. 45–47; E3, 2025, pos. 60–62). Data fragmentation and access problems were also highlighted, reflecting the issue of data silos (Sect. 2.1.5). Because they lacked a CRM system, data at C1 was scattered in Excel lists throughout the organization (E1, 2025, pos. 51). E4 (2025, pos. 16) confirmed that B2B clients often stored data in isolated silos across departments.

Another insight was the lack of structured historical data. E4 (2025, pos. 12) pointed out that even larger companies often need to start from scratch because they lack a consistent data history. This was confirmed by E5 (2025, pos. 17): "Historically, the data collection hasn't been excellent, so we are drawing on what metrics and dashboards we have available."

Technological Limitations

This subcategory was mentioned frequently, which suggests that issues related to technology remain a concern for experts. System integration problems were observed across companies of all maturity levels (E1, 2025, pos. 13; E2, 2025, pos. 12; E8, 2025, pos. 51). This included missing connections between third-party platforms such as LinkedIn and the CRM system, which resulted in the issue that generated leads occasionally were not transferred (E2, 2025, pos. 12) and outcomes had to be tracked manually (E10, 2025, pos. 4). Therefore, in practice, integration issues go beyond the core systems and include various systems and tools.

Another frequently cited problem was manual processes and a lack of or insufficient automation. This referred to lead management process stages (e.g., E10, 2025, pos. 12), and to reporting on outcomes (e.g., E8, 2025, pos. 51). Lead qualification, scoring, and nurturing often took place manually (E8, 2025, pos. 11; E10, 2025, pos. 12; E12, 2025, pos. 5). Similarly, reporting was frequently handled manually because of unsatisfactory capabilities of existing systems or the lack of automated dashboards (E8, 2025, pos. 11; E12, 2025, pos. 31). These issues were less frequently mentioned in companies with a high lead management maturity level. However, some experts had experienced similar problems in the past when lead management was "driven out of Excel files and Google Sheets and documents" due to the lack of marketing automation and standard operating models (E7, 2025, pos. 45). These insights are consistent with findings in the literature, which recognizes that many companies do not automate their lead management processes. In a recent study conducted in the DACH region, the average maturity level in lead management automation was only 36 out of 100 points. However, individual sectors, such as technology and service providers, performed slightly better (Zumstein et al., 2024, p. 3). The companies with the highest maturity and largely automated processes also operated in these sectors, apart from one company that was active in the manufacturing industry (Sect. 3.2.1).

Overall, this chapter has demonstrated that the interviewed companies face a wide variety of challenges in lead management, as summarized in Fig. 3.2.

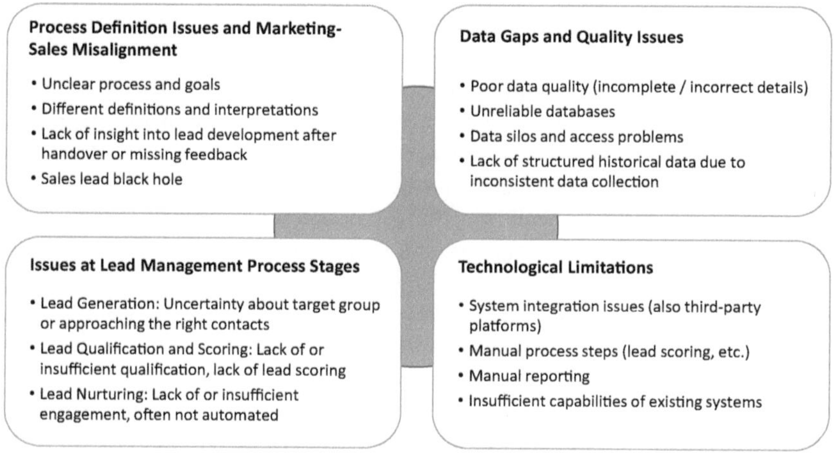

Fig. 3.2 Challenges and Bottlenecks in Lead Management. (Source: Own depiction based on the expert interviews)[4]

Frequently, these issues are interconnected. For example, the lack of an appropriate technological infrastructure can cause data silos and impair data quality. Some issues were fundamental and aligned with the literature. These include unclear process definitions, misalignment between marketing and sales, and poor databases. Experts frequently mentioned technological limitations, which seemed less of an issue in companies with a higher maturity level. However, even for these companies, problems remained, especially concerning system integration.

Additionally, companies faced different challenges in the lead management process stages. The conceptual framework described marketing analytics as an option for addressing these challenges. Therefore, the next section presents use cases of how marketing analytics can tackle issues at the lead management process stages identified in this section (see bottom left rectangle in Fig. 3.2). This

[4] The overview reflects interviewee responses and is therefore not exhaustive.

also includes how lead management effectiveness is measured, which can contribute to addressing the lack of insights into lead development after handover. However, issues regarding the overall process definition, data, and technology are often more fundamental and therefore cannot be solved by marketing analytics alone.

3.3 Marketing Analytics in B2B Lead Management

Considering the different maturity levels and various challenges described in the previous chapter, it became apparent that a universal approach for integrating marketing analytics into B2B lead management is not feasible. Nevertheless, marketing analytics offers improvements for the lead management process stages and effectiveness measurement. Following the discussion of marketing analytics in the conceptual framework, this chapter covers three areas:

- Marketing analytics applications: Present use cases of how companies apply data insights in lead generation, scoring, and nurturing to support decisions and improve activities.
- Performance measurement: Explore how companies measure lead management effectiveness, including relevant metrics and methods.
- Extent of data-driven decision-making: This dimension was added to assess if companies base their lead management decisions on data as opposed to intuition or experience.

3.3.1 Applications at Process Stages

For this chapter, the following subcategories were derived: *lead generation*, *lead scoring*, and *lead nurturing*. No separate category was created for lead handover because the interviews did not provide sufficient evidence for how this could be improved in a data-driven manner. A separate subcategory for *predictive analytics and Artificial Intelligence* was used to assess the opinions of the experts on this topic. Many of the following use cases refer to companies with a high maturity level in Wenger's model. This is likely because these companies have a more sophisticated technological infrastructure and clear process definitions compared to other companies with less mature processes.

3.3.1.1 Lead Generation

As shown in Sect. 3.2.3, some companies faced difficulties in defining or reaching their target group. This chapter describes examples from expert interviews on how companies use marketing analytics in practice to address this issue.

One expert acknowledged that they had traditionally run lead generation campaigns with broad, untargeted messages and only analyzed the suitability of the target group afterwards. However, they were trying to "flip that narrative [...] through data-driven analytics" earlier in the process (E7, 2025, pos. 54–55). Therefore, they examined regional market and industry characteristics and identified relevant accounts before launching campaigns to better address and engage them. They also wanted to focus on industries with strong potential (E7, 2025, pos. 54). These measures align with the target group analysis and market research described in Sect. 2.3.1.

Other experts directly mentioned the use of buyer personas. One company had created specific personas, which allowed them to develop tailored campaigns that aligned with the needs and language of these specific roles (E5, 2025, pos. 30–31). E8 (2025, pos. 25–29) described a workshop held at their company, which involved reviewing personas and job titles from the CRM system that represented successful leads for the company. They used these descriptive insights to tailor future campaigns and address the pain points, tasks, and needs of these personas. This way, they wanted to make sure to capture relevant leads (E8, 2025, pos. 25–27). The marketing department also incorporated feedback from inside sales regarding personas or company types into campaigns to only address relevant target groups (E8, 2025, pos. 36–37).

Another expert explained the need to standardize personas. The company had set up messaging documents for campaign targeting that included concrete buyer personas (E2, 2025, pos. 15). Although a particular persona was crucial to some of the company's activities, they had not previously defined this role within their systems. Therefore, they could not determine how many of these individuals were reached through lead generation campaigns. They worked on standardizing this role to track and target the audience better in the future (E2, 2025, pos. 17).

Another approach that had not been considered in the theoretical section involved identifying potential customers on the website, which is the primary source of leads for many companies (Philipp, 2021, p. 203). Two experts described the use of a tool that helped them identify companies that visited their website (E11, 2025, pos. 6; E12, 2025, pos. 11). One expert referred to Dealfront (E11, 2025, pos. 6), a sales and marketing intelligence platform for European

B2B companies (Dealfront, n. d.). Tools like Dealfront can be used to track IP addresses and distinguish between private individuals and business contacts who visit the website (Gebhardt & Gebhardt, 2019, p. 81). The tools show which pages and content were viewed and provide information like the size of the company and general contact details. However, specific decision-makers must be identified through additional research (Beck, 2025, p. 55; Gebhardt & Gebhardt, 2019, p. 81). Both companies leveraged the data provided by the tools to carry out SEA activities or initiate cold calling directed at the identified companies (E11, 2025, pos. 6; E12, 2025, pos. 11). However, the experts did not specify whether they further narrowed down the outreach to specific decision-makers.

Marketers can also use marketing automation to track the click paths of potential customers on the website and determine what they are interested in. This helps create personalized offers that encourage potential customers to provide their contact details (Rougemont & Terstiege, 2022, p. 118). In this context, another expert described an approach that could be realized with marketing automation and further integrations (E4, 2025, pos. 22; HubSpot, n. d.-b; n. d.-a). The expert discussed the possibility of conducting automated checks to determine whether a company visiting the website fits the target group. If so, suitable decision-makers could be identified automatically via LinkedIn. This data could be used for more precise targeting directed at specific contact persons and likely result in more relevant contacts (E4, 2025, pos. 25–26).

This subcategory showed how companies use insights from data to improve targeting. In addition to developing ICPs and buyer personas, experts explained that it is crucial to continuously analyze and standardize existing profiles. Furthermore, companies that use their website as a lead source can apply tools that help identify visitors and approach decision-makers directly. The generated leads must then be qualified, as discussed in the next section.

3.3.1.2 Lead Scoring

This subcategory describes how data insights are used to improve lead scoring. Even though the companies employed various approaches to lead qualification, lead scoring was frequently mentioned. Although lead scoring was only used by four companies, others planned to implement it in the future (E3, 2025, pos. 11–14) or expressed an interest in introducing it (E12, 2025, pos. 28–29). These experts hoped that lead scoring would allow them to better qualify leads for sales and assess their value (E3, 2025, pos. 22; E12, 2025, pos. 25). Against this backdrop, this analysis focuses on lead scoring as part of lead qualification.

Most lead scoring models described by the experts were traditional, rule-based models automated via marketing automation platforms. The models considered different criteria. One expert described an explicit lead scoring model based on demographic and firmographic information. They used a combination of a letter score to assess the fit of the company profile and a numerical score that considered the profile of the contact. If both were suitable, the lead was automatically forwarded to the CRM system (E2, 2025, pos. 4). The company had introduced several models for different business units. They discovered that, depending on the product area, decision-makers from different hierarchical levels were involved in purchasing decisions. Lead scoring models had to reflect these differences (E2, 2025, pos. 17). Additionally, the expert mentioned the intent data platform 6sense. The platform was occasionally used to identify accounts that are not a good fit for the company profile but show a high level of buying intent for a product. However, the expert was not sure if the tool was still applied (E2, 2025, pos. 10). 6sense is an AI-driven revenue intelligence platform (6sense, n. d.). It uses AI and predictive analytics to analyze large volumes of intent data, which includes demographic data, behavioral signals, and activities such as concrete product searches. Based on this, it can recognize patterns that indicate a high purchase probability and identify promising leads (A. Kaiser, 2024). Although E2 did not confirm it, the capabilities of 6sense suggest that the company occasionally supports its lead scoring process with predictive elements.

Another company used an implicit lead scoring model based on the lead's behavior to "catch people who are secretly very interested" (E5, 2025, pos. 27). Leads received points for activities, such as filling out a form or downloading content. When a certain number of points had been accumulated, the lead was contacted by sales (E5, 2025, pos. 27). According to the expert, lead scoring, together with other changes in lead nurturing (Sect. 3.3.1.3), had contributed to higher lead quality, time savings, and more Opportunities (E5, 2025, pos. 43).

As recommended in the literature, another company combined implicit and explicit elements in a scoring and grading model. In the past, the company had based lead scoring only on the lead's behavior. However, this could result in individuals being classified as high-priority leads even though they did not fit the buyer persona. Therefore, the company introduced a grading component, which evaluated the persona or job profile of each lead in addition to the behavior (E7, 2025, pos. 17–19).

The scoring model of the last company was also based on implicit and explicit components. However, they had to manually set check marks in the CRM system to increase the score. Still, the introduction of lead scoring had been helpful, because it ensured that the right leads were processed by inside sales employees and increased their efficiency (E8, 2025, pos. 6–9; 64–71).

The agency expert added that lead scoring was often used to focus on leads that currently show high engagement. This is relevant in industries with long sales cycles, such as mechanical engineering, because marketing can identify when companies become active again. According to the expert, lead scoring should not only be applied to individual contacts but to the overall company to identify relevant developments early (E4, 2025, pos. 22).

Two experts also described the need to adjust scoring models (Sect. 2.3.2). One company reviewed conversion data by job functions and market segmentations every month to determine if scoring thresholds needed to be increased or lowered (E2, 2025, pos. 15). The expert considered lead quality more critical than lead volume: "We look at our lead scoring and we make decisions and say, okay, we understand that these decisions are going to reduce the volume of leads, but it's going to increase the quality of leads" (E2, 2025, pos. 24). The changes the company recently made, i.e., the adjustment of thresholds, resulted in reduced volume of leads who qualified for sales (−31% volume compared to the previous quarter), but a significantly higher conversion rate (+90%), which indicates higher lead quality (E2, 2025, pos. 21). E7 observed a similar development following the changes made by adding the grading component to their model: "Our lead volume has significantly dropped, but the quality has grown dramatically" (E7, 2025, pos. 29). Even though the number of leads who qualified decreased, more leads converted, and Opportunities moved faster through the funnel (E7, 2025, pos. 29).

Table 3.3 summarizes the lead scoring models, the adjustments made, and the impact of the implementation or the changes to the models as described by the experts.

Table 3.3 Overview of Lead Scoring Models and Adjustments

Input Variables	Automated / Manual	Adjustments	Impact
Explicit	Automated (Marketing Automation)	Different models per business unit, continuous adjustments based on conversion data	Changes: Lower lead volume, higher conversion rate, and higher lead quality
Implicit	Automated (Marketing Automation)	Recent implementation together with automated lead nurturing workflows	Implementation: Higher lead quality, more sales opportunities, time saved
Combined (Explicit and Implicit)	Automated (Marketing Automation)	Addition of a grading component, continuous adjustment and further development	Changes: Lower lead volume, more leads converted, faster progression of Opportunities
Combined (Explicit and Implicit)	Manual (CRM System)	Recent implementation	Implementation: Processing the "right" leads, increased sales efficiency

Source: Own depiction based on the expert interviews[5]

This category has confirmed that lead scoring is an important element of lead qualification. For some companies, its introduction would already be possible based on their technological infrastructure (e.g., E3, 2025, pos. 12). However, this would require high-quality content and multiple touchpoints that leads can engage with (E3, 2025, pos. 12).

Companies that implemented lead scoring mostly used traditional models. Although one expert indicated the occasional use of predictive elements, this was not explicitly confirmed. This is consistent with the literature, which states that predictive models are rarely used in practice. Reasons for this could be the need for high data quality and availability, as well as know-how (Sect. 2.3.2). Three companies automated their lead scoring via marketing automation. Based on the literature and expert statements, a combination of explicit and implicit criteria is appropriate. In adjusting their models regularly, the experts prioritized

[5] The overview reflects interviewee responses and is therefore not exhaustive.

the quality of leads over quantity. Lead scoring usually occurs in parallel with lead nurturing, as described below.

3.3.1.3 Lead Nurturing

This subcategory describes how data insights are used to improve lead nurturing. It was coded less frequently than the previous subcategories, which is likely because many companies had not established lead nurturing processes yet. The challenges regarding lead nurturing (Sect. 3.2.3) were primarily because of its absence. However, different experts planned to introduce automated lead nurturing workflows or described them as a goal (E6, 2025, pos. 4; E8, 2025, pos. 31; E12, 2025, pos. 15). The existing marketing automation functions of some CRM systems would already enable this (E3, 2025, pos. 22; E12, 2025, pos. 9).

Some companies used lead nurturing strategies but had not implemented automated workflows. One company applied a newsletter system and planned to establish automated nurturing workflows with the introduction of a new CRM system. The goal was to hand over more concrete leads, because the current approach was not sufficiently effective (E10, 2025, pos. 34–36).

Even though another company used a marketing automation platform and lead scoring, they only applied generic messaging in nurturing (E7, 2025, pos. 23): "Nothing was really designed in the past around a targeted nurture path" (E7, 2025, pos. 23). Instead, leads were nurtured with general news and content. However, there were concrete plans to target leads based on their past behavior, industry, and company background in the future. For this, the company wanted to make use of progressive profiling (E7, 2025, pos. 21). They also employed a chatbot, but this was rather used to help individuals navigate the website than to nurture them. However, they planned to involve agent AI in the future to communicate with leads via emails to "provide that progressive […] nurture path and be predictive" (E7, 2025, pos. 27).

Other companies had already built automated lead nurturing workflows within marketing automation platforms. One expert explained that in the past, they had directly contacted potential customers after the first download of a whitepaper. Given stricter data protection requirements and the experience that leads often did not want to be contacted directly, they built up automated workflows to engage leads. Direct contact was only made when at least three nurturing steps (e.g., whitepaper, blog post, webinar) had been completed (E11, 2025, pos. 12–14).

The literature discusses the importance of personalization in lead nurturing. Another company applied a personalized nurturing approach via their marketing automation platform (E5, 2025, pos. 7). Using the example of a thematic workflow that sent the lead different industry or product content based on their interests, the expert described how the introduction of these processes had improved their lead nurturing. The workflow revolved around an e-book, a popular asset of the company. In the past, when a person requested the e-book, follow-up from marketing and sales had not been consistent. To improve this, the company established a largely automated process that guides the individual through different paths (E5, 2025, pos. 21; 23).

After the e-book form submission, leads were categorized based on firmographic characteristics and their buying intent as indicated by behavioral data (e.g., email opens, speed of engagement). High-intent leads who engaged quickly and had a high lead score received a follow-up message with access to additional assets. Medium-intent leads who engaged slowly or only partially received access to educational content and blogs. The goal was to clarify their interests and track their behavior to collect information that supports sales in reaching out later. Low-intent leads who did not download the e-book or had inadequate firmographic data received lower priority and were placed in long-term nurturing lists (E5, 2025, pos. 21).

The expert concluded: “And all of this collection, I think, gives us a lot more that we can do with each lead, and a lot more accurate placement within the funnel than we could before” (E5, 2025, pos. 21). They gained concrete insights into lead behavior and could engage them in the funnel in a personalized way (E5, 2025, pos. 23). The expert confirmed that these new processes, together with lead scoring, had resulted in better lead quality presented to sales. In addition, it led to a higher success rate for sales, because they had a better basis to contact individuals who had demonstrated actual interest (E5, 2025, pos. 43–45).

The agency expert implemented workflows via the platform HubSpot together with B2B clients (E4, 2025, pos. 22).[6] According to this expert, the possibility to collect different behavioral signals was a key advantage of these platforms: “Just because someone visited the website doesn’t mean they’re interested. Several data streams then converge to indicate when things are getting really interesting” (E4, 2025, pos. 22). The goal was to reach potential customers with the right content or information at the right time and “to make it as easy as possible for everyone to stay in this lead pipeline […] to ultimately become a customer” (E4, 2025, pos. 22). The expert concluded that even single measures could lead to significantly more conversions, orders, and more suitable leads (E4, 2025, pos. 25–26). Another topic raised by E4 (2025, pos. 22) was the personalized display of content on a website based on the previous behavior of the individual, allowing

---

[6] A detailed description of the implementation of automated lead nurturing workflows via HubSpot can be found in Gasser & Mäder (2022, pp. 104–105).

for more targeted messages. As described in Sect. 2.3.3, this can involve the use of AI.

The examples of these experts made it clear that the introduction of data-driven processes has advantages in guiding leads towards sales readiness. Tracking the behavior of leads can be used to identify their interests and develop personalized communications. However, these approaches require the use of a marketing automation platform, which is not available to all companies. This shows that technological limitations can prevent the introduction of more advanced lead nurturing practices. Some companies adopted a generic lead nurturing approach but planned to move to a more behavior-based and personalized approach in the future.

3.3.1.4 Predictive Analytics and Artificial Intelligence

The evaluation of the previous subcategories suggests that descriptive analytics dominate, because the focus is on "what happened" rather than predictive or prescriptive insights. Nevertheless, some experts briefly commented on the role of predictive analytics and AI in lead management. When asked to what extent predictive analytics already played a role for B2B clients, the agency expert estimated that only around 2–3% of the agency's customers considered predictive approaches (E4, 2025, pos. 30). This is consistent with findings in the literature that suggest that advanced analytics is not broadly adopted (Sect. 2.2.1). There were indications regarding predictive elements in lead scoring at one company, even though the expert was unsure about its active use (Sect. 3.3.1.2). Additionally, one company planned to incorporate predictive elements into its lead nurturing strategies in the future (Sect. 3.3.1.3). As described in Sect. 2.2.1, a strong technological infrastructure with integrated systems and data sources, as well as a solid lead management process, are prerequisites for companies to consider predictive analytics and AI. Since both companies were previously assigned the highest lead management maturity level and had largely automated processes, it can be assumed that implementing advanced analytics is possible for them.

When asked about the use of AI in lead management, the agency expert emphasized that most B2B customers still rely on task automation (E4, 2025, pos. 28). This is consistent with a recent study that found that lead management is often not adequately automated in B2B companies, and only very few broadly use AI-based tools in their processes (Busenhart, 2024). The agency expert highlighted the advantage of solutions such as HubSpot that already integrate AI functions (Sect. 2.3.3). This could enable companies to go beyond a rule-based approach and make automated decisions (E4, 2025, pos. 28). E10 (2025, pos. 64–68), whose company planned to implement a new CRM system, hoped that the

AI components of this system would enable them to better evaluate the interest of leads and initiate suitable reactions.

Moreover, content creation was mentioned as a frequent use case of AI in marketing (E4, 2025, pos. 28, E11, 2025, pos. 41–44). One expert stated that the creation of all content formats, such as images and texts for blog posts, was heavily supported by AI at their company (E11, 2025, pos. 41–44). This content is ultimately also part of lead generation or nurturing activities. However, some experts expressed concerns related to AI in lead management. E8 (2025, pos. 73–74) emphasized that they did not yet consider such approaches due to data protection concerns: "We already work with AI in the company, but of course under very strict regulations [...]. And customer data is naturally not included" (E8, 2025, pos. 74). Another expert voiced concerns over the factual accuracy of AI, stating that it was often accompanied by errors that could not be detected. Therefore, human intervention remained necessary (E5, 2025, pos. 63–65).

Overall, the interviewed companies were still in the early stages of using predictive analytics and AI in lead management. Several experts did not refer to these advanced approaches at all, likely because many of the interviewed companies still dealt with more fundamental issues regarding task automation. Only one expert mentioned using a tool involving predictive analytics, which indicates that descriptive approaches dominate among the interviewed companies.

3.3.2 Measurement of Lead Management Effectiveness

After examples of marketing analytics at the stages of the lead management process have been introduced, this section addresses the measurement of lead management effectiveness. Three subcategories were developed: *relevant metrics and funnel performance management*, *revenue and revenue attribution*, and *reporting and dashboards*. The first subcategory was derived deductively and covers effectiveness metrics related to lead quantity, quality, and conversion rates, as well as funnel performance measurement (Sect. 2.3.4). In addition, the experts made statements on revenue and revenue attribution. This subcategory was developed inductively because it had not been discussed in the conceptual framework.

3.3.2.1 Relevant Metrics and Funnel Performance Management

Some experts discussed efficiency metrics or other indicators beyond the effectiveness metrics outlined in Sect. 2.3.4 (e.g., E6, 2025, pos. 24; E12, 2025, pos. 27). Among others, these included interaction metrics such as click or open rates, the cost per lead, sales cycle, and customer lifetime value, as summarized in Appendix 9 in the Electronic Supplementary Material.

The quantity of leads often serves as a starting point for assessing effectiveness. Many experts confirmed tracking the number of, for example, MQLs or Opportunities generated (E1, 2025, pos. 39; E3, 2025, pos. 36; E8, 2025, pos. 45; E12, 2025, pos. 31). Various experts monitored how many leads were generated by channel or activity to understand which ones to focus on (E1, 2025, pos. 31–37; E3, 2025, pos. 27–32). However, some companies were only in the process of collecting and evaluating relevant data (E11, 2025, pos. 20; E12, 2025, pos. 23–33). Since Wenger's maturity model does not reflect data tracking practices, this also affected a company that was previously assigned the highest maturity level.

Yet, experts emphasized that the focus should be on lead quality rather than quantity (E6, 2025, pos. 16; E12, 2025, pos. 33). The importance of conversion rates was mentioned across all interviews. As noted in Sect. 2.3.4, their use varies. Several experts referred to the conversion from MQL into leads at the final qualification level before a sale as a crucial quality indicator. For some, this was the MQL-Opportunity rate (E2, 2025, pos. 27; E7, 2025, pos. 33), while others referred to the MQL-SQL rate (E8, 2025, pos. 37; E11, 2025, pos. 24).[7] One company used an internal benchmark of 20% conversion from MQLs to Opportunities with international subsidiaries (E10, 2025, pos. 42).

Two experts emphasized the importance of tracking the development of leads and conversion rates along the marketing and sales funnel, which aligns with the concept of funnel performance management (Sect. 2.3.4). Since both experts described this approach in detail and explained how improvements were derived, these are presented below.

One company had defined detailed internal lead qualification levels as leads were processed by inside sales between marketing and sales. They tracked the cumulative lead status and followed up on lead quality by calculating various conversion rates (E8, 2025, pos. 21). This, for instance, included the MQL-TAL (Telesales Accepted Lead) rate, which reflected the lead quality assessment by inside sales, whether the lead would be processed or rejected (E8, 2025, pos. 37). These metrics were reviewed weekly to assess the progression and quality of leads, and to compare campaigns, channels, and content. Insights were used directly to optimize future strategies (E8, 2025, pos. 19; 37). However, all

[7] The internal terminology used to describe lead qualification levels varied among experts. For some, SQL was the last qualification level before a sale, and for others, Opportunities.

these measurements were conducted manually, for which the company had built a comprehensive Excel dashboard (E8, 2025, pos. 47).

Similarly, another expert emphasized the importance of "data-driven volume, watching them [leads] flow through, you know, a funnel, essentially [...]" (E7, 2025, pos. 51). According to the expert, this was also a useful starting point for companies that just began to build a dashboard. Conversion rates should be monitored across different stages to understand where most leads drop out of the funnel and derive potential for improvement (E7, 2025, pos. 51). In addition, the underlying reasons should be investigated, such as why leads drop off at the top of the funnel (for example, many students or private individuals are attracted) (E7, 2025, pos. 51). Therefore, campaigns should be evaluated "consciously and truthfully" to assess whether the target group was reached and relevant leads were generated (E7, 2025, pos. 51). Another example included assessing why leads were rejected by sales, highlighting the importance of sales feedback. These descriptions are consistent with Neumüller & Bigliel's recommendations, who stressed the need to examine the reasons why leads drop out of the funnel (Sect. 2.3.4). The expert further mentioned that characteristics of converting Opportunities, such as job titles and industries, should be analyzed to approach individuals with similar traits in the future (E7, 2025, pos. 51). It was argued that these measurements would help not only evaluate campaigns but also overall lead management effectiveness (E7, 2025, pos. 51).

The above considerations are summarized in Fig. 3.3, which is a further development of Fig. 2.4. This also includes insights from Sect. 3.3.1.2 regarding the adjustment of lead scoring models based on conversion data.

Fig. 3.3 Funnel Performance Management and Further Analysis. (Source: Own depiction based on the concept of Beco & Zeren (2023, p. 356) and the expert interviews)

Although conversion rates were considered an important indicator of lead quality, another expert emphasized that lead drop-offs were inevitable. She raised the importance of a quick handover to sales to ensure that leads were contacted promptly, and that the sales team was provided with the information needed to reach out (E5, 2025, pos. 37).

In the literature, importance has been attached to the quality aspect in measuring lead management effectiveness. As demonstrated in this section, expert interviews confirmed this. The use of funnel performance management, including the underlying reasons for developments, was considered a helpful method for optimizing lead management activities in practice.

3.3.2.2 Revenue and Revenue Attribution

Additionally, the experts stressed the importance of revenue and revenue attribution in the context of lead management effectiveness. Many experts described revenue from marketing-generated leads that ultimately became customers as a crucial or even the most important key figure for marketing in lead management (E2, 2025, pos. 27; E3, 2025, pos. 36; E4, 2025, pos. 32; E5, 2025, pos. 67). Even though not every company was able to connect leads to the revenue generated, this was a goal for the future for some (e.g., E12, 2025, pos. 25–27).

Several interviewees emphasized that lead management from a marketing perspective was less about individual campaign-related or interaction metrics and more about the actual generated revenue (E4, 2025, pos. 32; E5, 2025, pos. 67; E11, 2025, pos. 28). Some experts described these changes as the result of a learning process over recent years (E4, 2025, pos. 32; E11, 2025, pos. 28). As E5 (2025, pos. 67) noted: "I do want to emphasize that the end goal of all of this stuff is not opens or clicks or qualifications or anything. It's revenue […]." The agency expert observed a shift, as in the past, metrics such as click rates had played an important role for many B2B clients. While these were still relevant for campaign evaluations, they could not be used to assess overall lead management success, which was related to "what really came out of it" (E4, 2025, pos. 32). Another expert agreed, stating that marketing would need to be measured more effectively at the revenue level in the future, and in this respect, move closer to sales: "Marketing in general needs to focus more on measurability" (E11, 2025, pos. 30).

After conducting further research, this perspective coincides with the view of some authors in the literature. Wenger (2023, p. 482) emphasizes that marketers frequently focus on "vanity metrics"[8] such as impressions or click rates as collected through web or social media analytics. However, these do not show the contribution of marketing to revenue. Therefore, it is crucial to demonstrate the impact of marketing's activities on outcomes (Rackley, 2015, pp. 8–9).

In this context, one expert discussed the importance of revenue attribution for marketing campaigns (E5, 2025, pos. 49). Attribution models enable a holistic analysis of the customer journey and individual touchpoints (Gasser & Mäder, 2022, p. 52). They are used to determine the effectiveness of marketing measures per channel and campaign (von Focht, 2022, p. 83) and to assess what contribution to revenue was made (Gasser & Mäder, 2022, p. 52). On this basis, decisions can be made regarding the allocation of the marketing budget (Wedel & Kannan, 2016, p. 110). A detailed discussion of revenue attribution models is beyond the scope of this thesis, as it focuses on lead management effectiveness from a holistic perspective. However, a distinction is frequently made between static attribution models, such as "last click wins", in which the last touchpoint receives the conversion value, and dynamic models that use algorithms to evaluate the contribution of each touchpoint individually (von Focht, 2022, pp. 84–85). Dynamic models counteract oversimplification, a common issue with static models (Ahrholdt et al., 2023, p. 271). Various authors discuss static and advanced attribution models in detail for further reference (e.g., Ahrholdt et al., 2023, pp. 269–277; Bhatta, 2022; von Focht, 2022, pp. 84–85).

In practice, measuring the success of individual marketing activities remains challenging in B2B settings due to extended customer journeys, many touchpoints, and the integration of online and offline channels (Andersen et al., 2018, p. 4). One expert confirmed that it was frequently not possible to attribute revenue to a specific marketing activity because of interruptions or overlaps in the development of leads (E3, 2025, pos. 36). In this case, it was recommended to use other data, such as if campaigns had generated Opportunities, or if leads qualified (E5, 2025, pos. 49). The agency expert emphasized the advantages of solutions such as HubSpot, because they consolidated data in a single dashboard. This made it easy to follow the impact of marketing measures on sales and the revenue generated (E4, 2025, pos. 40).

Overall, this subcategory has shown that, according to various experts, marketing is increasingly moving from vanity metrics to outcome-oriented key figures in

[8] Vanity metrics are described as "metrics that make you look good to others but do not help you understand your own performance in a way that informs future strategies" (Tableau, n. d.).

lead management, particularly revenue. It was also argued that in the future, marketing needs to focus more on measuring its impact on revenue by demonstrating the value of its activities.

3.3.2.3 Reporting and Dashboards

A further subcategory was formed to show how experts reported on the metrics described in the previous subsections, as briefly discussed in Sect. 2.3.4. According to Krieger (2021, p. 153), clear reporting structures are crucial to monitor and improve the lead management process in the long term. Overall, three use cases could be derived from the interviews: automated reporting, manual reporting using Excel, and a lack of reporting structures. Regarding the first use case, most experts mentioned that relevant metrics were accessible via the CRM system, at least from the moment the lead was identified (E2, 2025, pos. 29; E5, 2025, pos. 51; E11, 2025, pos. 24). Several interviewees used BI platforms for deeper analysis of metrics, data visualization, and dashboard retrieval (E5, 2025, pos. 11; E10, 2025, pos. 22; E11, 2025, pos. 8). The prerequisite for this is the integration between CRM systems and BI tools (E2, 2025, pos. 29; E5, 2025, pos. 11; E10, 2025, pos. 22).

Some companies used manual reporting because their CRM system did not meet all their requirements. They created customized Excel dashboards and updated them manually to track campaigns and follow up on leads (E8, 2025, pos. 11–13; 46–47). One expert described this approach as inefficient: "Manual. Excel lists. Incredibly time-consuming" (E12, 2025, pos. 31). In addition, some companies had not yet established any reporting structures due to the lack of a marketing-oriented lead management process (E9, 2025, pos. 9).

Some experts noted that reporting structures and the creation and use of dashboards depended on the company and systems used, which made it challenging to derive best practices (E3, 2025, p. 54; E7, 2025, p. 51). This is consistent with statements in the literature (Klaus, 2023, pp. 447–448). One expert explained: "So, it's definitely different for every company, and Salesforce reporting is not the easiest. It's kind of like an art" (E7, 2025, pos. 51). One expert noted that real-time dashboards might not be helpful due to long sales cycles in B2B settings. At their company, it often took years for deals to materialize, making it difficult to track leads and assess the effectiveness of individual measures (E12, 2025, pos. 35–37). Nevertheless, it was noted that dashboards should be as simple and understandable as possible to alleviate concerns of employees about handling data (E1, 2025, pos. 57). Another expert recommended that separate dashboards should be created for different use cases (E3, 2025, pos. 54).

This subcategory showed that reporting processes and the use of dashboards varied widely between the interviewed companies. This is primarily due to the tools used and the technical capabilities available. Several experts emphasized the importance of integrating CRM systems with BI tools for deeper analyses. However, some companies still relied on manual reporting, causing efficiency problems.

Having covered practical applications of marketing analytics and effectiveness measurement, the next section concludes Chapter 3.3 with the extent of data-driven decision-making.

3.3.3 Extent of Data-Driven Decision-Making

As described in Sect. 2.2.1, data-driven decision-making involves relying on data and analytics when making decisions rather than intuition or gut feeling. Since the literature offers different perspectives on this topic, the experts were asked directly how they assessed the extent of data-driven decision-making in lead management in their marketing departments. It is important to note that these assessments reflect the subjective perception of experts.

Three experts stated that their decisions in lead management were based mainly on data insights. These companies had previously been assigned a high maturity level. E7 (2025, pos. 15) reported that lead management decisions were "100% dependent on data insights, and where we are right now has completely flipped and evolved from intuition and experience." However, the expert acknowledged that 20–30% of approaches should be experimental to test new methods for which data was not available (E7, 2025, pos. 57). Similarly, E2 (2025, pos. 15) stated that their lead management decisions were strongly based on data insights. The expert justified this with a monthly meeting, during which all leads generated in the previous month were reviewed in terms of conversion rates per job function, job category, and market segmentation. Based on this, they derived targeted improvements for the lead management process. However, intuitive elements still played a role, for example, when using messaging documents in the context of campaigns (E2, 2025, pos. 15). Another expert also described their work as data-driven, emphasizing that reports were regularly evaluated to assess the development of leads and derive decisions for future activities (E8, 2025, pos. 19).

Two experts stated they relied on a combination of experience and data insights for lead management decisions. E1 (2025, pos. 19) explained that they had managed to reduce intuitive decision-making to a minimum. Therefore, decisions either depended on experience or past and current data. Another expert considered a solid database as a prerequisite for data-driven decisions: "In order to be correctly data-driven, you need a good collection of data to analyze in the first place. And if you only started collecting your full set six months ago, then that kind of thing for analysis isn't going to cut it" (E5, 2025, pos. 17). The expert recognized that in some campaigns, intuition was necessary because there was sometimes no precedent. In addition, the experience of sales representatives in handling leads still played a significant role (E5, 2025, pos. 17).

The remaining experts relied largely on experience and intuition in lead management decisions. The experts from the two companies that did not yet have a marketing-oriented lead management process stated that decisions such as choosing topics for campaigns, the timing for campaigns, or selecting trade fairs were based on gut feeling or experience because they lacked relevant data. However, they expected that their future processes would enable them to make more data-driven decisions (E6, 2025, pos. 14–18; E9, 2025, pos. 17). Other reasons for relying on experience and intuition included the lack of relevant data at the top of the funnel, because leads were quickly passed to sales (E3, 2025, pos. 22), and a poor database and missing system integrations (E12, 2025, pos. 17). Another expert highlighted that decisions regarding target groups and campaign planning were based on experience and standards rather than data, because long B2B sales cycles complicated a data-driven strategy (E11, 2025, pos. 15–20). In addition, it was argued that "we somehow never had the capacity or the time to actually carry out this plan, do, check, act" (E4, 2025, pos. 20).

This is consistent with observations made by the agency expert, who emphasized that companies often set the goal of generating more leads, but do so based on gut feeling: "they should actually have this information at their fingertips and be able to say, 'this is how it's going here, this is how it's going there, [...] and we want 20% more here, 50% more there.' But a lot of it is still done based on gut feeling" (E4, 2025, pos. 12). The expert did not observe significant differences between industries regarding data-driven decision-making, but rather regarding the age and size of the company. According to the expert, younger companies often operate in a more networked manner and utilize data more effectively. Older companies are often hindered by data silos and internal data protection regulations, despite frequently having extensive and valuable data pools (E4, 2025, pos. 16).

Although three of the companies with a high lead management maturity level reported largely data-driven decision-making, two companies with a high maturity level stated that they relied on a combination of experience or intuition and data insights, or entirely on experience and intuition. This suggests that a high level of lead management maturity alone does not necessarily go hand in hand with data-driven decision-making. However, it was also acknowledged that some level of intuitive decision-making was still needed, for example, to account for the experience of sales representatives in handling leads, and if new strategies were carried out for the first time. Having discussed the practical use of marketing analytics in lead management in Sect. 3.3, the next section deals with the success factors for integration.

3.4 Success Factors for Integration

The subcategories for this chapter were formed directly from the interviews because of the limited availability of specific academic sources. Fig. 3.4 summarizes the five subcategories and the main findings, which are described in more detail below.

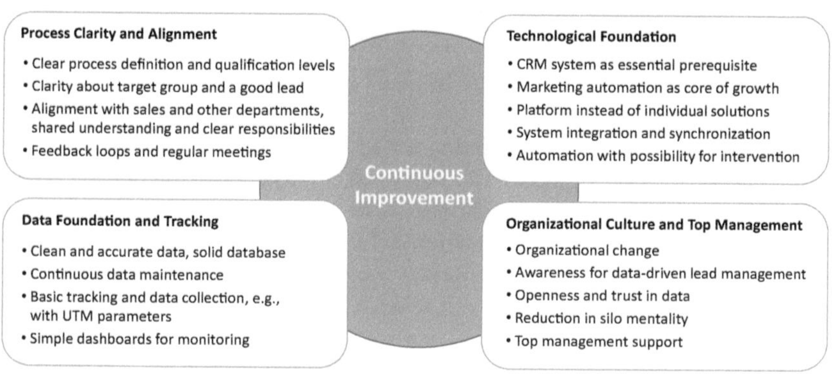

Fig. 3.4 Success Factors for Integrating Marketing Analytics Approaches. (Source: Own depiction based on the expert interviews)[9]

The recommendations were mainly discussed for companies that are just starting to implement marketing analytics in lead management. Several factors were linked to the challenges outlined in Sect. 3.2.3, especially *process clarity and alignment*, *technological foundation*, and *data foundation and tracking*. This suggests that fundamental issues must be addressed first. Another topic raised

[9] The overview reflects interviewee responses and is therefore not exhaustive.

was *organizational culture and top management involvement*, which is frequently addressed in the literature (Sect. 2.2.2). Furthermore, *continuous improvement* was a crucial insight. It was placed at the center of Fig. 3.4 because it builds on the other factors and also applies to companies that want to develop existing approaches further.

Process Clarity and Alignment

Many experts stated that clarity about the lead management process forms the basis. This includes basic lead qualification levels, the target group, and what constitutes a good lead (E3, 2025, pos. 51–52; E4, 2025, pos. 12; 38; E9, 2025, pos. 43). The importance of alignment with sales and other departments was confirmed again. In the first step, this meant "bringing everyone to the table" (E4, 2025, pos. 38; E6, 2025, pos. 40) to ensure shared understanding and clear responsibilities. Later, this included feedback loops and regular meetings between involved departments (E6, 2025, pos. 30; E11, 2025, pos. 2; E12, 2025, pos. 39). The agency expert concluded: "We need to have all these fundamentals in place before we take the next step [...]" (E4, 2025, pos. 14).

Technological Foundation

Furthermore, having the right tools in place allows to access data and metrics quickly and centrally (E8, 2025, pos. 57; E10, 2025, pos. 26). Many experts agreed that this required implementing a CRM system from the beginning (E1, 2025, pos. 51; E5, 2025, pos. 55; E8, 2025, pos. 58–59). This system had to function well, cover the basic data fields, and work for both marketing and sales (E3, 2025, pos. 50; E5, 2025, pos. 55). Interestingly, one expert argued that implementing a marketing automation platform was a more critical first step than a CRM system: "You can always implement a new CRM, but your marketing automation platform is going to be crucial as you grow and scale, and you don't want to switch that platform" (E7, 2025, pos. 49). The expert argued that this platform was the "automation driver" and should be chosen based on the company's goals and growth objectives (E7, 2025, pos. 49).

The agency expert recommended an enterprise platform like HubSpot or Salesforce instead of individual solutions. The expert argued that these enable faster and easier implementation of strategies, because they offer centralized data access and integrated analytics (e.g., website interactions, CRM data). There might be interface problems with individual solutions, because companies need to collect information from different sources (E4, 2025, pos. 23–24). The expert concluded: "If you have a lot of money, a lot of manpower, and a lot of time, you don't need a platform. If you don't have all of that, I would strongly recommend a platform" (E4, 2025, pos. 24). This was also a realistic goal for smaller companies because there are many different solutions available that companies can choose from (E4, 2025, pos. 41–42). Related to these recommendations was the need for integration and synchronization between systems to ensure continuous data flow (E7, 2025, pos. 36–37). However, for some experts, this was only a goal and not a reality (e.g., E9, 2025, pos. 57–59; E12, 2025, pos. 39).

As the previous chapters have shown, automation was a frequent topic in many interviews. Some experts emphasized that processes should be automated as much as possible to reduce manual workload and minimize errors, especially when handling many leads (E3, 2025, pos. 46; E10, 2025, pos. 40; 50). However, another expert who worked for a company that already had a high degree of automation noted that it was important not to automate everything, because manual intervention and data corrections were still necessary (E2, 2025, pos. 38).

Data Foundation and Tracking

Furthermore, the importance of a solid database was emphasized. This includes working with clean and accurate data from the beginning (E1, 2025, pos. 45–51) and a joint commitment with sales to data maintenance (E6, 2025, pos. 30). Sect. 3.2.3 showed that although a good database is essential for analytics, this was not the case in all companies. A first recommendation was: "Integrate tracking and data collection into everything you already have and just let it run [...] to actually have a database and something you can look at" (E4, 2025, pos. 38). Depending on the interactions and traffic, this should be done over several weeks (E4, 2025, pos. 38).

In this context, two experts recommended implementing "minimum possible tracking" by adding UTM parameters to URLs (E5, 2025, p. 54). These tracking parameters help identify the source or campaign the lead originated from and track them throughout the process. For this purpose, free tools such as UTM.io could be used (E3, 2025, pos. 4; 54). Another recommendation was: "Start by building very simple, ugly dashboards that you can track" (E5, 2025, pos. 59). This is useful to follow the current development of leads and compare them with the previous week, month, or year, depending on what data is available (E5, 2025, pos. 61).

Organizational Culture and Top Management Involvement

The topics identified in this subcategory correspond to the literature that often discusses the adaptation of organizational culture and top management involvement as prerequisites for marketing analytics (Länsipuro & Karjaluoto, 2021; Wedel & Kannan, 2016). Similarly, some experts emphasized the need for organizational change, which one expert described as most critical. The expert explained that the implementation of data-driven approaches depends on the age and size of the company and is easier at a small start-up company, because everything can be built from scratch. In older and larger companies, implementation is more difficult because established organizational processes and structures need to be changed (E7, 2025, pos. 43). This was confirmed by another expert, who emphasized that their company still had to develop an understanding of what data-driven lead management is (E12, 2025, pos. 39). Other topics mentioned include openness to new approaches, trust in data, and reducing silo mentality and departmental thinking (E4, 2025, pos. 34).

In the context of top management support, one interviewee described the benefit of having a "champion somewhere in higher management" who supported data collection and provided necessary resources (E5, 2025, pos. 55).

Continuous Improvement

Another crucial insight was the importance of continuous improvement. Several experts saw a common issue in striving for a perfect solution (E1, 2025, pos. 57; E2, 2025, pos. 34; E5, 2025, pos. 59). One expert observed that "the perfect becomes the enemy of the good," as marketers often focused on collecting lots of data and setting up a perfect technological infrastructure without addressing fundamental issues first (E5, 2025, pos. 59).

A clear definition of objectives and outcomes was seen as crucial: "Identify what the objective is and what you're trying to improve on, and measure that" (E2, 2025, pos. 34). This included compiling existing metrics and agreeing on how changes would be defined, such as what it means for the business to generate more leads (E4, 2025, pos. 38). To ensure buy-in from all departments, everyone should understand the rationale behind individual activities, such as lead nurturing, and why changes are needed (E2, 2025, pos. 32).

Companies should focus on getting started with small, basic steps and implement them quickly (E5, 2025, pos. 59–61; E7, 2025, pos. 55). Although one expert described this "move fast" mentality as culturally motivated ("a very American answer" (E5, 2025, pos. 59)), another expert also stated that speed was needed to act and react quickly (E4, 2025, pos. 34). In addition, companies should make incremental improvements: "Look at the data on a weekly, bi-weekly basis. Observe what the outcomes are and be comfortable with pivoting and making modifications as you go" (E2, 2025, pos. 34). Since there was no universal approach that always worked, companies should try out different approaches (E4, 2025, pos. 34). Therefore, measures had to be reported, analyzed, and optimized continuously as part of continuous improvement (E4, 2025, pos. 4).

This chapter has shown that fundamental factors must be implemented first to integrate marketing analytics into B2B lead management. Based on this, experts described continuous improvement as essential for the implementation and optimization of measures. This was mainly highlighted by companies with a high lead management maturity level and the agency expert.

Development of a Practical Guide 4

This chapter combines insights from the conceptual framework and the empirical findings to derive a practical guide. Table 4.1 presents a corresponding overview. Due to differences in maturity levels, the guide is a collection of recommendations rather than a universal solution. By reviewing the tables in each section, marketing professionals can get an overview of the addressed issues and recommendations to decide which ones suit their company's needs best. Further information about the individual measures can be found in the relevant chapters of the thesis, which are directly referenced at the beginning of each section.

Table 4.1 Overview Practical Guide

Purpose	Practical Steps and Recommendations for Integrating Marketing Analytics Approaches into B2B Lead Management to Improve Process Effectiveness
Target Group	B2B Marketing Professionals from Various Company Sizes and Industries
Scope	Lead Management Process Stages up to Lead Handover to Sales
Structure	Section 1: Laying the Foundations
	Section 2: Applying Marketing Analytics at Process Stages
	Section 3: Creating and Monitoring Metrics for Measuring Effectiveness
	Section 4: Continuous Improvement

Source: Own depiction

Supplementary Information The online version contains supplementary material available at https://doi.org/10.1007/978-3-658-50959-0_4.

L. Hannemann, *Integrating Marketing Analytics Approaches into B2B Lead Management*, BestMasters, https://doi.org/10.1007/978-3-658-50959-0_4

4.1 Section 1: Laying the Foundations

Before companies can start integrating marketing analytics into their lead management processes, they must lay the foundations.

Lead Management Maturity Assessment

This section builds on insights from Sects. 2.1.1 and 3.2.1. First, companies need to understand their maturity level in lead management, because this influences the ability to integrate marketing analytics approaches. Frameworks such as Wenger's maturity model can serve as a starting point for assessing lead management process maturity. Companies with low maturity levels from a marketing perspective (Levels 1 or 2 in Wenger's model) should first focus on fundamental issues. This includes process clarity, terminology, and the definition of lead qualification levels. Considering the lack of software support at these levels, a crucial requirement is the implementation of a CRM system to avoid data fragmentation and ensure centralized data access. Further recommendations on the general setup of lead management processes can be found in the literature (e.g., Vossebein et al., 2024).

Companies with defined lead management processes (Level 3 in Wenger's model) have these fundamentals in place and can focus on developing established processes, for example, by improving lead qualification. If marketing automation is not available, companies should expand their lead management core infrastructure accordingly. This can be realized through the implementation of an enterprise platform that comprises a CRM and marketing automation function, via add-ons, or with integrations. To assess readiness regarding automation, companies can use models such as the "Marketing Automation Maturity Index (MAMI)" (Zumstein et al., 2023).

Companies with a high process maturity, as reflected in a separate lead management department or a team within marketing (Level 4 in Wenger's model), are characterized by clear responsibilities and process steps. They use well-integrated software that ensures continuous data flow and end-to-end measurement of leads. While companies at lower maturity levels should focus on descriptive analytics, these companies can consider further developing existing processes with advanced analytics or AI applications.

In addition to these factors, Wenger's model considers the relationship between marketing and sales. Companies with undefined or unaligned relationships should improve the alignment between the functions, including a shared definition of responsibilities and goals (e.g., qualification criteria for a sales-ready lead) and agreement on metrics and objectives.

Success Factors for Integration

Establishing a foundation with lead management process clarity and alignment, as described above, is a fundamental prerequisite. However, companies should consider additional factors. This section combines insights from Sects. 2.1.5, 2.2.2, 3.3.3, and 3.4. An overview is provided below, while Appendix 10 in the Electronic Supplementary Material contains further details. Depending on the maturity level and the sophistication of marketing analytics applications, not all factors are equally relevant, or further requirements may be necessary, as detailed in later sections. In general, companies are advised to start with descriptive analytics and only move to AI support and predictive analytics once the prerequisites in terms of a solid lead management process, data quality, systems integration, and technologies are fulfilled.

As described above, a CRM system is a central prerequisite for data-driven lead management. It should function well and cover basic data fields. As Sects. 4.2 and 4.3 will show, basic analytics applications can also be implemented without marketing automation (e.g., manual lead scoring via the CRM system). However, the technological infrastructure should ideally comprise marketing automation, because it serves as an important enabler of marketing analytics and facilitates various analytics applications with automated processes.

In general, systems, including third-party platforms, should be integrated well to ensure end-to-end tracking and data flow. This guide does not provide tool recommendations or prerequisites for implementation, since these depend on the company's circumstances and can be consulted in the literature (e.g., Körner, 2021). Compared to individual solutions, an enterprise platform has the advantage that data can be accessed centrally. To increase efficiency, automation is helpful both in supporting process stages, such as lead nurturing, and reporting on outcomes. Nevertheless, there should be options for manual intervention to identify and correct mistakes in data. The core infrastructure for lead management can be supported by further analytics tools in the realm of web or social media analytics, especially at the top of the funnel.

The availability of clean and accurate data is important for analytics integration. To ensure data quality, a shared commitment with sales to data maintenance is recommended. In addition, companies should gain an overview of relevant data types and sources. Companies with poor historical data collection or those just starting with data-driven approaches must first establish a solid database. A useful starting point is to run data collection for some time and start with simple tracking, for example, via UTM parameters. Additionally, companies may have to adhere to data protection regulations in their lead management and analytics efforts.

Furthermore, companies should foster a corporate culture that embraces marketing analytics. This includes encouraging trust in data and openness towards data-driven approaches while reducing "silo mentality" and departmental thinking. As alignment between marketing and sales remains crucial, regular meetings between both departments and other stakeholders involved are recommended. This also includes feedback loops regarding lead quality (Sect. 4.3). Top management support is an additional enabler for marketing analytics in lead management.

Overall, companies differ in their data-driven decision-making in lead management. Therefore, they should reflect on the extent to which marketing relies on data and analytics versus intuition or gut feeling when making lead management decisions. Although experience and intuition remain necessary in some situations, such as when executing strategies that do not have a precedent or experience from sales representatives is needed, this can be a starting point to assess which strategies to focus on. Once companies are aware of their prerequisites and success factors, they can turn to concrete marketing analytics applications.

4.2 Section 2: Applying Marketing Analytics at Process Stages

Companies face a variety of challenges in lead management that are sometimes fundamental and cannot be solved by marketing analytics alone. However, data insights can help address common issues in the lead management process stages, as presented below.

Improving Targeting in Lead Generation

This section combines insights from Sects. 2.3.1 and 3.3.1.1. A common issue in lead generation is the insufficient targeting of potential customers. This can include a lack of clarity regarding the target group or broad, untargeted messages. Companies can counteract this by knowing their audience and addressing potential customers most likely to buy to generate relevant leads. Corresponding best practices are summarized in Table 4.2.

Table 4.2 Recommendations for Lead Generation

Common Issues	Insufficient targeting of potential customers (e.g., lack of clarity about target group, broad messages)
Analytics Solution	Target group analysis and identification
Development and Application of ICPs and Buyer Personas	Develop target customer profiles: ICPs (company level) and buyer personas (decision-makers) using data insights (quantitative or qualitative analyses)
	Continuously analyze successful buyer personas and job titles to derive insights for future campaigns (workshops), including feedback from sales
	Examine regional market and industry characteristics and identify relevant accounts before launching campaigns to better address and engage them
	Standardize important personas within systems to track them better
	Outcome: Lead generation campaigns tailored to the needs and preferences of valuable potential customers, choose suitable channels, capture relevant leads
Outlook: Predictive Analytics and AI Support	Leverage AI-driven tools and predictive analytics to develop ICPs or buyer personas
	Outcome: Uncover and predict patterns that could indicate future demand
Identification of Potential Customers	Use tools (e.g., Dealfront) to identify website visitors, search for decision-makers via LinkedIn (possibly supported by marketing automation and further integrations)
	Outcome: Targeted outreach to generate more relevant leads

Source: Own depiction based on Sects. 2.3.1 and 3.3.1.1

A first step is to develop precise profiles at the company level (ICPs) and the decision-maker level (buyer personas). This requires analyzing historical data in the CRM system and can be accompanied by qualitative insights from interviews. Mature companies with a solid database can use predictive analytics or AI-driven tools to support the development of profiles. The advantage of precise profiles is that potential customers can be targeted based on their needs and preferences. This increases the likelihood of successful campaigns and the choice of channels that appeal to the target group. Once such profiles have been developed, they can be used as a basis for further analyses. This includes conducting market analyses before launching campaigns to identify relevant accounts beforehand. Another useful approach is conducting regular workshops to review the characteristics of successful personas and job titles in the CRM system and derive insights for the development of future campaigns. This ensures that the right target groups are reached, and their needs and pain points are addressed. Feedback from sales regarding personas or company types is also valuable in this context. To track how many relevant leads were generated by campaigns, companies should standardize important personas in the CRM or marketing automation system.

The identification of anonymous potential customers is another helpful approach for targeted communication. As the website is the most important source of leads for many companies, tools like Dealfront can be used to reveal which companies have visited the website and what content they were interested in. Based on this, lead generation measures can be directed at the identified company. An even more targeted approach is achieved by searching for specific decision-makers, for example, via LinkedIn, and addressing them individually. With the help of marketing automation and further integrations, such an approach can be automated.

Optimizing Evaluation and Prioritization with Lead Scoring

The findings in this section compile insights from Sects. 2.3.2 and 3.3.1.2. A common issue at the lead qualification stage is the lack of lead evaluation or the reliance on intuition. This can result in low-quality leads being handed over to sales. Companies can prevent this issue by developing lead scoring models that are adjusted continuously, as shown in Table 4.3.

Table 4.3 Recommendations for Lead Scoring

Common Issues	Lack of or insufficient evaluation and prioritization of leads, reliance on intuition
Analytics Solution	Lead scoring model implementation and adjustment
Traditional Lead Scoring	Establish a rule-based lead scoring model based on explicit (demographic and firmographic) and implicit (behavioral) criteria
	Automate lead scoring and adapt models per business unit
	Continuously adjust and refine the lead scoring model based on data insights (e.g., conversion data) and prioritize lead quality over volume
	Outcome: Better lead quality presented to sales, increased conversion rates, increased efficiency in sales (focus on relevant leads), and more sales Opportunities
Outlook: Predictive Lead Scoring	Set up an ML-based lead scoring model that uses predictive analytics to calculate propensity scores (e.g., via AI-driven revenue intelligence platforms)
	Outcome: Decreased bias and misconception, increased effectiveness

Source: Own depiction based on Sects. 2.3.2 and 3.3.1.2

Implementing lead scoring models ensures that better lead quality is presented to sales, conversion rates are increased, and sales can focus their efforts on relevant leads. However, in practice, companies might not use lead scoring, for example, because they lack the technological infrastructure. Another prerequisite is sufficient and accurate lead data, because building models on poor data can impair their effectiveness, and high-quality content for leads to engage with. Companies just starting with such approaches should focus on traditional models and use insights from various reports for setup (e.g., Adobe, 2020). Explicit (firmographic and demographic) and implicit (behavioral) criteria should be combined to achieve the best outcomes. If automation is not possible, lead scoring can be conducted manually, for example, by setting check marks in the CRM system. However, companies should try to automate the lead scoring process using marketing automation due to its better capabilities regarding behavioral tracking and higher efficiency. It is recommended to develop scoring models per business unit to account for different decision-makers, even though this is not feasible for every company.

If companies use traditional models, monthly reviews and adjustments, together with sales, are crucial. Various analyses should be carried out to adjust criteria, raise or lower scores, or adapt the scoring threshold. For example, conversion data by different criteria, such as job functions, can be reviewed, or the differences between rejected leads and leads that became Opportunities can be evaluated. These adjustments are often a trade-off between lower lead volumes versus higher conversion rates and increased lead quality. Decisions should be made in a way that prioritizes lead quality.

Even though predictive lead scoring is becoming a frequently discussed approach, its application in practice is limited. Such models require high-quality data and are difficult to implement. Nevertheless, companies that have already built an automated lead scoring model with explicit and implicit criteria and have the required data quality and know-how in place should consider supporting it with predictive elements. Compared to traditional models, where marketers must set rules for the scoring model, these models reduce bias and misconception. This can, for instance, be achieved via AI-driven revenue intelligence platforms such as 6sense.

Enhancing Engagement and Personalization in Lead Nurturing

This section builds on Sects. 2.3.3 and 3.3.1.3. A common issue in lead nurturing is the lack of engagement or the absence of a consistent strategy, resulting in generic communication. Companies can counteract this by implementing personalized nurturing strategies (Table 4.4).

Table 4.4 Recommendations for Lead Nurturing

Common Issues	Lack of or inconsistent engagement of leads, generic messages
Analytics Solution	Personalized lead nurturing
Consistent Lead Nurturing Strategy	Implement other ways of relationship building if marketing automation is not available, e.g., events, personalized email marketing
Lead Nurturing Workflows	Establish automated workflows via marketing automation to engage leads with the right content or information at the right time
	Make use of progressive profiling and behavioral tracking
	Outcome: More possibilities to engage leads, more qualified leads, higher conversion rates, and higher success rates for sales
Outlook: AI in Lead Nurturing	AI-supported marketing automation, automatic campaign optimization, and personalized content on websites
	Outcome: Even more targeted and personalized engagement

Source: Own depiction based on Sects. 2.3.3 and 3.3.1.3

Personalization is essential to provide leads with relevant content at the right time and develop them towards a purchase. In this context, lead nurturing recommendations often relate to the availability of a marketing automation platform, which is not the case for every company. In addition, personalization requires clearly defined processes and high-quality data. If these requirements are not fulfilled, companies should use alternative ways of building relationships with leads, such as hosting events or applying personalized email marketing. In any case, a personalized approach that aligns with the interests and preferences of the lead is important.

If possible, companies should use options provided by marketing automation to gather information about the lead's behavior, interests, industry, and company background to send them through targeted paths. This can be achieved by setting up automated workflows based on predefined triggers and through progressive profiling. Depending on the lead's stage in the customer journey, different workflows are relevant. These approaches can contribute to more qualified leads, higher conversion rates, and a higher success rate for sales, as leads are engaged according to their needs while relevant information about them is collected.

To achieve even more targeted engagement, companies that have already implemented marketing automation and respective workflows can consider resorting to AI support. This might, for example, include AI-driven campaign optimization within the marketing automation platform by automatically improving the frequency and timing of nurturing emails. AI can also help display personalized content on the website based on the past activities of leads to ensure increased engagement and more relevant contacts.

4.3 Section 3: Creating and Monitoring Metrics for Measuring Effectiveness

Once companies have implemented marketing analytics approaches in the lead management process stages, they must measure the effectiveness of their efforts. This involves identifying the most relevant metrics, tracking their contribution against objectives over time, and using the results to improve marketing's performance. This section describes how these steps can be implemented in practice. The approaches discussed build on Sects. 2.3.4 and 3.3.2.

Identify and Track Relevant Metrics

Companies might face issues in measuring lead management effectiveness from a marketing perspective. For instance, they might rely on intuition rather than data when selecting campaigns or channels. Companies can counteract this issue by identifying and tracking relevant metrics. In this context, Table 4.5 summarizes relevant best practices.

Table 4.5 Recommendations for Identifying and Tracking Relevant Metrics

Common Issues	Reliance on intuition rather than data (e.g., when selecting campaigns or channels), poor effectiveness measurement
Analytics Solution	Identify relevant metrics and monitor them against objectives over time
Prerequisites	Metrics and objectives defined jointly by marketing and sales
	Regular feedback from sales on the quality of marketing-generated leads
	Reporting structure (ideally automated)
Metrics Examples	Lead quantity (e.g., number of leads generated per channel and campaign), quality and conversion rates by lead qualification stage
	Other metrics: efficiency indicators (e.g., cost per lead), lead velocity, etc.

Source: Own depiction based on Sects. 2.3.4, 3.3.2.1 and 3.3.2.3

The selection of metrics depends on the company and its objectives. Some authors provide comprehensive lists that can serve as a basis (e.g., Beco & Zeren, 2023). However, marketing should focus on a few key metrics defined jointly with sales. The metrics must be tracked continuously to derive improvements, although the frequency depends on individual requirements. In addition, companies should establish clear reporting structures. Depending on the infrastructure, reporting can be automated, for example, via CRM systems and BI integrations. This allows for deeper analyses and dashboard visualizations. Another possibility includes manual reporting via Excel. Due to the effort involved, this should only be considered if the technological infrastructure is missing or existing systems do not cover all requirements. Once these prerequisites are in place, companies can start selecting relevant metrics.

For companies that rely on intuition in building campaigns and selecting channels, a useful starting point is determining the quantity of leads generated by channel and campaign. The availability of this data is important to define lead generation targets and know which campaigns, sources, or content are most effective at generating leads. However, it is also crucial to know whether the right leads are generated. Conversion rates play an important role in assessing lead quality and can be measured at different stages of lead development. This can, for instance, include the MQL-SAL rate, which indicates the quality of leads transferred to sales, or the rate of leads that become Opportunities (e.g., MQL-Opportunity rate). Another important metric is how many and which MQLs turned into customers. Since lead qualification levels differ internally, companies must define their own lead quality metrics. These indicators should be considered at the campaign, channel, and content level to assess activities in lead generation and nurturing and improve accordingly. Overall, lead quality should play an important role in measuring effectiveness. In this context, marketing should receive feedback from sales to understand whether MQLs fulfill quality criteria, as described in the next section.

Implement Funnel Performance Management

Another frequent issue, also for mature companies, is the lack of end-to-end measurement of leads and missing insights into their development after handover. To understand which measures are effective, marketing must know how leads develop and whether they have become customers. Funnel performance management is an approach that can serve as a starting point for dashboard development and should be implemented jointly with sales (Table 4.6).

Table 4.6 Recommendations for Funnel Performance Management

Common Issues	Lack of end-to-end measurement capability and missing insights into further development of leads after handover to sales
Analytics Solution	Implement funnel performance management
Prerequisites	Marketing and sales funnel jointly managed by marketing and sales
	Consistent measurement of metrics
Implementation	Track lead development in the funnel, including conversion rates and drop-off points
	Understand the underlying reasons for development and optimize accordingly
	Monthly meetings between marketing and sales to review leads generated in the past month (e.g., conversion data), derive targeted adjustments to the process
	Implement feedback loops with sales to receive feedback on lead quality
	Outcome: Better visibility of lead development, adjust and optimize measures

Source: Own depiction based on Sects. 2.3.4 and 3.3.2.1

Funnel performance management helps track relevant metrics over time and use the results to derive improvements. In this context, the development of leads, including quantity and conversion rates, should be tracked along the stages of the funnel. Such an approach helps to identify bottlenecks and derive areas for improvement. Marketers can see where leads drop out of the funnel and investigate the reasons behind these developments. They can ask questions such as: Why do leads drop off at the top/middle/bottom of the funnel? Why were leads rejected by sales? What are the characteristics of converting Opportunities?

Tracking lead progression through the funnel helps assess the effectiveness of campaigns, channels, and content in lead generation and nurturing, and adjust future strategies accordingly. It also helps to assess whether the right target group was reached and relevant leads were generated to improve targeting. Additionally, as described previously, lead scoring models can be adjusted based on conversion data. Funnel performance management ultimately helps companies assess the overall effectiveness of lead management. If the funnel is managed jointly by marketing and sales, this ensures that marketing has insight into the further development of leads after handover. Companies just starting to collect relevant data can begin by building simple dashboards to compare the development of leads against the previous week, month, or year, depending on what data is available.

A useful best practice is conducting monthly meetings with sales to review the development of leads generated in the past month. In this context, different data, such as conversion rates by job functions or category, can be discussed. Based on this, targeted adjustments can be derived for the lead management process. Furthermore, sales should provide feedback on every lead forwarded, especially on the reasons why it was or was not accepted (e.g., poor target group fit, not yet sales-ready). Such a feedback process should be standardized and kept as simple as possible (e.g., different predefined buttons that can be selected), possibly implemented via email or the CRM system.

Revenue and Revenue Attribution

The revenue from leads generated by marketing that became customers is considered a crucial metric. This is needed to demonstrate the added value of marketing activities and allocate the budget. Still, marketing may focus on vanity metrics rather than revenue contribution. As shown in Table 4.7, companies can use revenue attribution models to counteract this.

Table 4.7 Recommendations for Revenue Attribution

Common Issue	Focus on vanity metrics instead of revenue contribution
Alternatives to Revenue Attribution Models	If revenue attribution is not possible, focus on other data, e.g., Opportunities generated, qualified leads
Implement Attribution Models	Implement static attribution models
	Use advanced attribution models
	Outcome: Demonstrate marketing's contribution to revenue

Source: Own depiction based on Sects. 2.3.4 and 3.3.2.2

While vanity metrics are still relevant to campaign evaluations, they cannot be used to assess lead management effectiveness from a marketing perspective. Revenue attribution plays an important role in assessing which marketing activities have contributed to revenue. In this context, businesses can use attribution models. Even though static models are an option, it is recommended to move to advanced models to avoid oversimplification. While recommendations for attribution models are beyond the scope of this guide, companies can find further information elsewhere (e.g., Ahrholdt et al., 2023). However, due to long sales cycles and multiple touchpoints, revenue attribution remains a difficult task for many companies. If attribution is not feasible, companies can start reviewing alternative data, such as whether campaigns generated Opportunities or if leads qualified. Enterprise platforms offer advantages because they enable a holistic view of the impact of marketing measures and the revenue generated.

While the recommendations in this guide focus on effectiveness outcomes, companies should also consider efficiency metrics such as the cost per lead or new customer. In addition, individual metrics such as lead velocity and the customer lifetime value might be considered.

4.4 Section 4: Continuous Improvement

When integrating marketing analytics approaches into lead management, it is advisable to follow the general steps as described in this section. The content builds on a central finding from Sect. 3.4. Overall, marketers should make continuous improvements to their processes rather than striving for perfection. The literature offers various models for implementing continuous improvement processes. A simple instrument is Plan, Do, Check, Act (PDCA), which can be applied to various issues (Posluschny, 2025, pp. 67–69). A detailed theoretical explanation of this model is beyond the scope of this guide. However, companies can use the model to make incremental improvements to their lead management processes, regardless of whether they plan to implement a new step or improve an existing one.

In the *Plan phase*, it is necessary to define objectives that should be achieved. In this context, everyone involved should have the same understanding of the desired change and understand the reasoning behind it, for instance, why lead scoring is necessary and why changes are needed. In the *Do phase*, it is recommended to start with small, basic steps and implement them quickly. This speed is necessary to act and react quickly. During the *Check phase*, marketers can look at the data on a weekly or bi-weekly basis and make incremental modifications. As part of the *Act phase*, the change can be standardized and a new improvement initiated (Posluschny, 2025, pp. 67–70).

A concrete example of the application of PDCA could be as follows: A company realizes that too many low-quality leads are being passed to sales and plans to introduce a traditional lead scoring model based on explicit and implicit criteria to ensure that high-quality leads are handed over (Plan). The model is introduced via the marketing automation platform (Do). After evaluating conversion rates, some leads receive a high score but still do not convert. The company adjusts the weights of some scoring criteria (Check). The new scoring methodology is adopted, and conversion rates and other data are reviewed continuously (Act).

Overall, this guide can be ended with the following advice:

> *"No lead management practices are going to be perfect. So don't strive for perfection and just try something, do something, make an improvement, and fail fast. [...] Because the goal here [...] is continuous improvement [...]."* (E2, 2025, pos. 34)

Conclusion and Outlook 5

This section summarizes the main findings of the thesis in the light of the research questions, discusses the contributions to theory and practice, and the limitations and future directions.

5.1 Summary of Key Findings

The purpose of this thesis was to answer the following research question: How can marketing analytics approaches be integrated into B2B lead management to make processes more effective? For this purpose, two sub-questions were derived. They investigated the key challenges and bottlenecks that hinder effectiveness and explored how marketing analytics insights can optimize specific process stages (SQ1), and which metrics and success factors are required for integrating marketing analytics approaches into lead management processes (SQ2).

The conceptual framework demonstrated that lead management is an important approach for B2B companies to generate new potential customers and develop them into actual customers. Against the backdrop of digital customer journeys, marketing plays an increasingly important role in addressing potential customers, qualifying and prioritizing them for sales, and developing them towards sales readiness. In this process, however, companies are confronted with a wide variety of challenges. Even though some issues are fundamental, marketing analytics, defined as the process of applying marketing data to generate insights for decision-making and performance optimization, can assist in addressing common problems.

L. Hannemann, *Integrating Marketing Analytics Approaches into B2B Lead Management*, BestMasters, https://doi.org/10.1007/978-3-658-50959-0_5

The empirical findings from interviews showed that companies in practice exhibit major differences in lead management maturity from a marketing perspective. While some companies were only just beginning to involve marketing in the lead management process, others had already established largely automated and standardized process flows. In this context, numerous challenges and bottlenecks were identified, for instance, relating to the process definition, the alignment between marketing and sales, data gaps, and technological limitations. These differences have made it clear that a universal solution for the integration of marketing analytics approaches into B2B lead management is neither feasible nor purposeful.

Regarding the optimization of process stages as part of SQ1, the analysis confirmed that companies frequently face challenges related to the inadequate targeting of potential customers, a lack of or insufficient lead qualification, and a missing or inconsistent lead nurturing strategy. To address these issues, different applications of marketing analytics were presented. In lead generation, companies can improve targeting by conducting target group analysis and identification. This involves developing precise target customer profiles and constantly using insights from analyses to enhance campaigns, channels, and content. In addition, companies can ensure targeted outreach through website visitor identification. Furthermore, to enhance the lead quality presented to sales, companies can implement lead scoring models, ideally combining explicit and implicit criteria. Based on data insights, these models should be adjusted continuously. In lead nurturing, marketing analytics can assist in building personalized engagement strategies based on behavioral tracking to better develop leads towards sales readiness. All approaches ultimately seek to contribute to improved lead quality and increased conversion rates. In each area, depending on their prerequisites, companies can implement approaches of varying complexity, ranging from descriptive to predictive and AI-supported approaches.

In the context of SQ2, it was found that even though the approaches to effectiveness measurement depend on the company's needs, important metrics are related to lead quantity and, crucially, lead quality, as frequently reflected in conversion rates along the marketing and sales funnel. In this context, funnel performance management is a helpful approach that, if managed jointly with sales, helps marketing increase the visibility of the progression of leads. By understanding the reasons behind developments in the funnel, marketing can adjust and optimize activities in lead generation and nurturing, as well as the lead scoring model. In addition, the need to shift from vanity metrics towards measuring revenue and revenue attribution is increasingly needed to demonstrate the actual impact of marketing activities on outcomes.

To integrate marketing analytics approaches into B2B lead management, it has become clear that companies must first establish fundamental prerequisites. This especially includes lead management process clarity and alignment between marketing, sales, and other departments involved. Even though companies can start with basic approaches, a solid technological and data foundation and an organizational culture that encourages data-driven decision-making are important success factors. Depending on the sophistication of analytics approaches the company wants to pursue, different factors may become relevant. For example, leveraging AI and predictive analytics requires a solid lead management process, a well-integrated technological infrastructure, a strong connection of data sources, as well as high-quality data.

Ultimately, the importance of continuous improvement became clear. Companies should start with small, quick steps and make incremental improvements to their processes.

5.2 Contributions to Theory and Practice

Overall, the analysis in this thesis was complicated by several factors, particularly due to varying maturity levels and differences in the involvement of marketing, the use of technology, and the degree of automation. These differences became evident during the expert interviews and resulted in a variety of challenges, complicating the possibility of developing a standard solution. Nevertheless, the thesis bridged the identified theoretical and practical gap by strategically combining the fragmented literature related to marketing analytics and B2B lead management and expanding and refining these findings with insights from the expert interviews.

As for the theoretical contribution, findings from various research areas were consolidated to create a robust conceptual framework for the integration of marketing analytics into lead management. Instead of concentrating on advanced analytics, the thesis deliberately considered approaches in the field of descriptive analytics and automation. This is because in practice, companies still struggle with task automation (Busenhart, 2024), as confirmed by the interviews (Sect. 3.2.3). While contributions frequently focus on lead management process stages in isolation (e.g., lead scoring), this thesis provided a broad perspective by considering lead generation, lead scoring, lead nurturing, and the alignment between marketing and sales.

The thesis empirically validated and refined the variety of lead management maturity levels and the various challenges identified in the literature. In addition, the theoretical framework for marketing analytics applications at different lead management process stages was expanded and enriched with concrete use cases. This also applies to metrics and approaches for effectiveness measurement. In addition, the thesis established a deeper understanding of the success factors required to integrate marketing analytics into B2B lead management.

Practically, this thesis contributed with the development of a concise, practical guide for B2B marketing professionals. The guide provides the fundamental prerequisites and success factors that companies should address to integrate marketing analytics approaches. Depending on the issues marketers want to address, the guide offers use cases of varying complexity for lead generation, scoring, and nurturing. These approaches can be selected and implemented depending on the company's needs and prerequisites. At the same time, the guide's target group receives guidance and recommendations on how to measure the effectiveness of their efforts and improve processes continuously. More in-depth information can be found by referring directly to the relevant chapters in the thesis.

5.3 Limitations and Future Directions

As explained in the introduction, although the role of sales at the interface with marketing and the alignment between the two functions were considered, the scope of the thesis was limited to the marketing perspective in lead management. Therefore, apart from the importance of feedback processes, steps after the handover to sales were not investigated in depth. In order to analyze the customer journey holistically at the company level, future work could adopt a perspective that includes the steps that sales teams carry out to ultimately close a deal. Although this thesis addressed the alignment between marketing and sales in various process steps, future studies could focus more specifically on the handover of leads between marketing and sales.

Furthermore, even though efficiency aspects were considered in terms of the extent to which they influence effectiveness, the focus was on effectiveness-oriented improvements. Future research could further explore the impact of integrating marketing analytics in B2B lead management on efficiency, for example, by analyzing cost per lead or ROI in more detail.

The empirical part comprised a qualitative study in the form of expert interviews. Even though a homogeneous sample of twelve experts was used that represented different company sizes and industries, which allowed in-depth analyses of individual cases and revealed recurring and contrasting themes, the results cannot be generalized statistically. This is a limitation of the qualitative research methodology in itself (Helfferich, 2022, p. 890).

Lastly, this thesis primarily focused on descriptive methods and possibilities of rule-based automation. This approach was justified by the limited adoption of AI and predictive analytics in lead management practice, as confirmed in the literature (e.g., Vossebein et al., 2024; Zumstein et al., 2024) and the expert interviews (Sect. 3.3.1.4). Even though introduced and compared with more basic applications (e.g., traditional and predictive lead scoring models), advanced analytics was not investigated in depth. Due to the opportunities offered by AI and predictive analytics in lead management, including deeper analyses of customer data, better prediction of their behavior, and increased personalization, it can be assumed that these approaches will play an important role in the future (Vossebein et al., 2024, p. 45; Zumstein et al., 2024, p. 3). Even though the thesis has demonstrated that companies can start with more basic approaches in the realm of descriptive analytics, other studies could explore potential use cases and prerequisites of AI and predictive analytics in lead management in more depth.

References

6sense. (n. d.). *6sense—The ABM Platform Powered by Revenue Intelligence*. Retrieved July 14, 2025, from https://6sense.com/

Adobe. (2020). *The definite guide to lead scoring*. Adobe. https://business.adobe.com/content/dam/dx/us/en/resources/guides/lead-scoring/lead-scoring.pdf

Agag, G., Shehawy, Y. M., Almoraish, A., Eid, R., Chaib Lababdi, H., Gherissi Labben, T., & Abdo, S. S. (2024). Understanding the relationship between marketing analytics, customer agility, and customer satisfaction: A longitudinal perspective. *Journal of Retailing and Consumer Services, 77*. https://doi.org/10.1016/j.jretconser.2023.103663

Agarwal, U. A. (2019). Qualitative Interviewing. In R. N. Subudhi & S. Mishra (Eds.), *Methodological Issues in Management Research: Advances, Challenges, and the Way Ahead* (pp. 79–91). Emerald Publishing Limited. https://doi.org/10.1108/978-1-78973-973-220191006

Agnihotri, R., Afshar Bakeshloo, K., & Mani, S. (2023). Social media analytics for business-to-business marketing. *Industrial Marketing Management, 115*, 110–126. https://doi.org/10.1016/j.indmarman.2023.09.012

Ahrholdt, D., Greve, G., & Hopf, G. (2023). *Online-Marketing-Intelligence: Erfolgsfaktoren, Kennzahlen und Steuerungskonzepte für praxisorientiertes Digital-Marketing*. Springer Fachmedien. https://doi.org/10.1007/978-3-658-40599-1

Albrecht, M., & Schlüter, T. (2022). Customer Journey Analytics. In M. Halfmann & K. Schüller (Eds.), *Marketing Analytics: Perspektiven – Technologien – Anwendungsfelder* (pp. 195–214). Springer Fachmedien. https://doi.org/10.1007/978-3-658-33809-1_11

Andersen, P., Archacki, R., De Bellefonds, N., & Ratajczak, D. (2017). *How digital leaders are transforming B2B marketing*. Boston Consulting Group. https://web-assets.bcg.com/img-src/BCG-How-Digital-Leaders-Are-Transforming-B2B-Marketing-Apr-2017_tcm9-152916.pdf

Andersen, P., Archacki, R., Mustaghi, B., & Premo, R. (2018). *Building an Integrated Marketing and Sales Engine for B2B*. Boston Consulting Group. https://web-assets.bcg.com/img-src/BCG-Building-an-Integrated-Marketing-and-Sales-Engine-for-B2B-June-2018-NL_tcm9-196057.pdf

Baker, S. E., & Edwards, R. (2012). *How many qualitative interviews is enough? Expert voices and early career reflections on sampling and cases in qualitative research*.

L. Hannemann, *Integrating Marketing Analytics Approaches into B2B Lead Management*, BestMasters, https://doi.org/10.1007/978-3-658-50959-0

National Centre for Research Methods. https://eprints.ncrm.ac.uk/id/eprint/2273/4/how_many_interviews.pdf

Basu, R., Lim, W. M., Kumar, A., & Kumar, S. (2023). Marketing analytics: The bridge between customer psychology and marketing decision-making. *Psychology & Marketing, 40*(12), 2588–2611. https://doi.org/10.1002/mar.21908

Beck, M. (2025). Phase 1 im Vertriebszyklus: KI bei Lead-Generierung und -Qualifizierung. In M. Beck (Ed.), *Künstliche Intelligenz im Vertrieb: KI-Lösungen für jede Phase des Verkaufszyklus: Einsatzmöglichkeiten, Tools und Implementierung* (pp. 49–59). Springer Fachmedien. https://doi.org/10.1007/978-3-658-46433-2_3

Beco, J., & Zeren, E. (2023). Funnel Performance Management. In U. Hannig & U. Seebacher (Eds.), *Marketing and Sales Automation: Basics, Implementation, and Applications* (pp. 347–360). Springer International Publishing. https://doi.org/10.1007/978-3-031-20040-3_22

Bhatta, I. (2022). Optimizing Marketing Channel Attribution for B2B and B2C with Machine Learning Based Lead Scoring Model [Ph.D., Capitol Technology University]. In *ProQuest Dissertations and Theses*. https://www.proquest.com/docview/2716520342/abstract/6D7C02D149A4099PQ/1

Bogner, A., Littig, B., & Menz, W. (2014). *Interviews mit Experten: Eine praxisorientierte Einführung*. Springer Fachmedien. https://doi.org/10.1007/978-3-531-19416-5

Brummer, J. (2024, May 16). *Marketing Automation: Ein umfassender Leitfaden*. https://blog.hubspot.de/marketing/was-ist-marketing-automatisierung

Bucholtz, M. (2000). The politics of transcription. *Journal of Pragmatics, 32*(10), 1439–1465. https://doi.org/10.1016/S0378-2166(99)00094-6

Busenhart, C. (2024, March 27). *Lead Management by Companies Not Sufficiently Automated*. ZHAW School of Management and Law. https://www.zhaw.ch/en/sml/about-us/press-news/newsdetail/event-news/lead-management-by-companies-not-sufficiently-automated

Click. (2024, June 9). *Click | Automatisierte Marketing-Tools für das Wachstum Ihres Unternehmens*. https://clickdimensions.com/de/

Cogan, M., & Orgis, H. (2021). KI-gestützte Leadgenerierung im B2B-Marketing. In M. Terstiege (Ed.), *KI in Marketing & Sales – Erfolgsmodelle aus Forschung und Praxis: Konzepte und Instrumente zum erfolgreichen Einsatz künstlicher Intelligenz* (pp. 203–224). Springer Fachmedien. https://doi.org/10.1007/978-3-658-31519-1_13

Cooper, M. J., & Budd, C. S. (2007). Tying the pieces together: A normative framework for integrating sales and project operations. *Industrial Marketing Management, 36*(2), 173–182. https://doi.org/10.1016/j.indmarman.2006.03.005

Dach, C. (2023). *Inbound-Marketing für B2B-Unternehmen: Neukunden digital gewinnen*. Springer Fachmedien. https://doi.org/10.1007/978-3-658-42262-2

Davenport, T. H., Guha, A., & Grewal, D. (2021). How to Design an AI Marketing Strategy: What the technology can do today—And what's next. *Harvard Business Review, July–August 2021*. https://hbr.org/2021/07/how-to-design-an-ai-marketing-strategy

Dealfront. (n. d.). *Die Go-to-Market-Plattform für Europa*. Retrieved July 2, 2025, from https://www.dealfront.com/de/platform/

DeepL. (n. d.). *Home – DeepL*. Retrieved April 26, 2025, from https://www.deepl.com/de/home

Delen, D., & Demirkan, H. (2013). Data, information and analytics as services. *Decision Support Systems, 55*(1), 359–363. https://doi.org/10.1016/j.dss.2012.05.044

Delen, D., & Zolbanin, H. M. (2018). The analytics paradigm in business research. *Journal of Business Research, 90*, 186–195. https://doi.org/10.1016/j.jbusres.2018.05.013

Deszczyński, B. (2016). The Impact of Opportunity Management on the Relationship Business Model (A Study in the Polish Housing Industry). *Journal of Eastern European and Central Asian Research (JEECAR), 3*(2). https://doi.org/10.15549/jeecar.v3i2.137

D'Haen, J., & Van den Poel, D. (2013). Model-supported business-to-business prospect prediction based on an iterative customer acquisition framework. *Industrial Marketing Management, 42*(4), 544–551. https://doi.org/10.1016/j.indmarman.2013.03.006

D'Haen, J., Van den Poel, D., Thorleuchter, D., & Benoit, D. F. (2016). Integrating expert knowledge and multilingual web crawling data in a lead qualification system. *Decision Support Systems, 82*, 69–78. https://doi.org/10.1016/j.dss.2015.12.002

Dresing, T., & Pehl, T. (2018). *Praxisbuch Interview, Transkription & Analyse: Anleitungen und Regelsysteme für qualitativ Forschende* (8th ed.). Published Independently.

Espadinha-Cruz, P., Fernandes, A., & Grilo, A. (2021). Lead management optimization using data mining: A case in the telecommunications sector. *Computers & Industrial Engineering, 154*. https://doi.org/10.1016/j.cie.2021.107122

Eurostat. (n. d.). *Glossary: Enterprise size*. Eurostat. Retrieved June 28, 2025, from https://ec.europa.eu/eurostat/statistics-explained/index.php?title=Glossary:Enterprise_size

Fantini, F., & Narayandas, D. (2023). *Analytics for Marketers: When to rely on algorithms and when to trust your gut*. Harvard Business Review. https://hbr.org/2023/05/analytics-for-marketers

Farrugia, B. (2019). WASP (Write a Scientific Paper): Sampling in qualitative research. *Early Human Development, 133*, 69–71. https://doi.org/10.1016/j.earlhumdev.2019.03.016

Fili, J., Alt, D., Katzenberger, L.-S. K., Christoph, S., & Piazza, A. (2025). Einsatz von Künstlicher Intelligenz im B2B Customer-Relationship-Management: Identifikation von Herausforderungen und Einsatzpotenzialen in produzierenden kleinen und mittleren Unternehmen. *HMD Praxis der Wirtschaftsinformatik, 62*(1), 134–152. https://doi.org/10.1365/s40702-024-01132-w

Gartner. (n. d.). *Definition of Artificial Intelligence (AI)—Gartner Information Technology Glossary*. Gartner. Retrieved May 10, 2025, from https://www.gartner.com/en/information-technology/glossary/artificial-intelligence

Gartner. (2020). *Gartner Reveals More Than Half of Marketing Leaders Are Disappointed in Their Analytics Results*. Gartner. https://www.gartner.com/en/newsroom/press-releases/2020-10-07-gartner-reveals-more-than-half-of-marketing-leaders-a

Gasser, M., & Mäder, L. (2022). *Automation von Marketing und Sales für B2B-Unternehmer: Mithilfe der digitalen B2B-Roadmap den Umsatz steigern*. Springer Fachmedien. https://doi.org/10.1007/978-3-658-36859-3

Gebhardt, M. (2023). Lead-Scoring bei B-to-B-Unternehmen – Eine Bestandsaufnahme. *Marketing Review St. Gallen, 40*(5), 68–77.

Gebhardt, M., & Gebhardt, L. (2019). Datenbasierte Ansätze der Lead-Generierung. *Marketing Review St. Gallen, 36*(5), 76–82.

General Secretariat of the Council. (n. d.). *The general data protection regulation*. Consilium Europa. Retrieved March 14, 2025, from https://www.consilium.europa.eu/en/policies/data-protection-regulation/

Germann, F., Lilien, G. L., & Rangaswamy, A. (2013). Performance implications of deploying marketing analytics. *International Journal of Research in Marketing, 30*(2), 114–128. https://doi.org/10.1016/j.ijresmar.2012.10.001

González-Flores, L., Rubiano-Moreno, J., & Sosa-Gómez, G. (2025). The relevance of lead prioritization: A B2B lead scoring model based on machine learning. *Frontiers in Artificial Intelligence, 8*. https://doi.org/10.3389/frai.2025.1554325

Google Analytics. (n. d.). *Jetzt zu Google Analytics 4 wechseln*. Retrieved July 25, 2025, from https://support.google.com/analytics/answer/10759417?hl=de

Greiner, R., Berger, D., & Böck, M. (2022). *Analytics und Artificial Intelligence: Datenprojekte mehrwertorientiert, agil und nachhaltig planen und umsetzen*. Springer Fachmedien. https://doi.org/10.1007/978-3-658-38159-2

Halfmann, M. (2022). Marketing Analytics – Trend oder Zukunft? In M. Halfmann & K. Schüller (Eds.), *Marketing Analytics: Perspektiven – Technologien – Anwendungsfelder* (pp. 3–14). Springer Fachmedien. https://doi.org/10.1007/978-3-658-33809-1_1

Hallikainen, H., Savimäki, E., & Laukkanen, T. (2020). Fostering B2B sales with customer big data analytics. *Industrial Marketing Management, 86*, 90–98. https://doi.org/10.1016/j.indmarman.2019.12.005

Hannig, U. (2021). Lead Management Automation vereint Marketing und Vertrieb. In U. Hannig (Ed.), *Marketing und Sales Automation: Grundlagen – Umsetzung – Anwendungen* (pp. 243–257). Springer Fachmedien. https://doi.org/10.1007/978-3-658-21688-7_17

Heinzelbecker, K. (2021). CRM, CXM und Marketing Automation. In U. Hannig (Ed.), *Marketing und Sales Automation: Grundlagen – Umsetzung – Anwendungen* (pp. 135–147). Springer Fachmedien. https://doi.org/10.1007/978-3-658-21688-7_10

Helfferich, C. (2022). Leitfaden- und Experteninterviews. In N. Baur & J. Blasius (Eds.), *Handbuch Methoden der empirischen Sozialforschung* (pp. 875–892). Springer Fachmedien. https://doi.org/10.1007/978-3-658-37985-8_55

Hilgenstock, E., & Kuhle, P. (2022). Künstliche Intelligenz im B2B-Vertrieb – Mensch und Maschine: Ein Dream-Team? *Digitale Welt, 6*(4), 56–58. https://doi.org/10.1007/s42354-022-0552-8

Honka, A., & Durst, C. (2025). Ideal Customer Profile, Customer Insights und Buyer Personas – Kenne deine Kunden. In C. Durst (Ed.), *B2B Digital Marketing Playbook: Strategie – Toolbox – Best Practices* (pp. 31–53). Springer. https://doi.org/10.1007/978-3-658-45379-4_3

HubSpot. (n. d. -a). *Connect HubSpot and LinkedIn Sales Navigator*. Retrieved July 12, 2025, from https://knowledge.hubspot.com/integrations/how-to-connect-hubspot-and-linkedin-sales-navigator

HubSpot. (n. d. -b). *Leitfaden zur DSGVO-konformen Nutzung von HubSpot*. Retrieved April 25, 2025, from https://www.hubspot.de/data-privacy/gdpr/hubspot-product-playbook

HubSpot. (n. d. -c). *Track website visits*. Retrieved July 12, 2025, from https://knowledge.hubspot.com/prospects/use-prospects

HubSpot. (2025). *The State of Marketing: Data-driven growth tactics and emerging trends to guide marketers into an AI-first business landscape*. HubSpot Inc. https://www.hubspot.com/state-of-marketing

Huttelmaier, H., & Heigl, J. (2023). Boosting Marketing and Sales Automation's Effectiveness: Strategies to Increase Lead Quality. In U. Hannig & U. Seebacher (Eds.), *Marketing and Sales Automation: Basics, Implementation, and Applications* (pp. 297–315). Springer International Publishing. https://doi.org/10.1007/978-3-031-20040-3_19

Huttelmaier, H., Hesselbach, N., & Heigl, J. (2022). *Stand von Marketing Automation 2022: Einsatz und Nutzung in deutschen Unternehmen.* https://doi.org/10.57714/h41w-2h59

Iacobucci, D., Petrescu, M., Krishen, A., & Bendixen, M. (2019). The state of marketing analytics in research and practice. *Journal of Marketing Analytics, 7*(3), 152–181. https://doi.org/10.1057/s41270-019-00059-2

IBM. (2024, October 1). *What is Data?* https://www.ibm.com/think/topics/data

Jadli, A., Hain, M., & Hasbaoui, A. (2023). Artificial intelligence-based lead propensity prediction. *IAES International Journal of Artificial Intelligence (IJ-AI), 12*(3), 1281–1290. https://doi.org/10.11591/ijai.v12.i3.pp1281-1290

Jain, A. (2024, January 16). *How to Define Your Ideal Customer Profile (ICP) for Precision Targeting.* Gartner. https://www.gartner.com/en/digital-markets/insights/b2b-ideal-customer-profile

Järvinen, J. (2016). *The Use of Digital Analytics for Measuring and Optimizing Digital Marketing Performance* [Jyväskylä University School of Business and Economics]. https://jyx.jyu.fi/jyx/Record/jyx_123456789_51512#:~:text=The%20findings%20confirm%20that%20digital,insights%20to%20continuously%20improve%20results.

Järvinen, J., & Taiminen, H. (2016). Harnessing marketing automation for B2B content marketing. *Industrial Marketing Management, 54*, 164–175. https://doi.org/10.1016/j.indmarman.2015.07.002

Kaiser, A. (2024, June 13). *Understanding and Using Intent Data.* https://6sense.com/platform/intent-data/what-is-intent-data/

Kaiser, R. (2021). *Qualitative Experteninterviews: Konzeptionelle Grundlagen und praktische Durchführung.* Springer. https://link.springer.com/book/10.1007/978-3-658-30255-9

Khodakarami, F., & Chan, Y. E. (2014). Exploring the role of customer relationship management (CRM) systems in customer knowledge creation. *Information & Management, 51*(1), 27–42. https://doi.org/10.1016/j.im.2013.09.001

Kiron, D., Ferguson, R. B., & Kirk Prentice, P. (2013). From Value to Vision: Reimagining the Possible with Data Analytics. *MIT Sloan Management Review, 54*(3). https://sloanreview.mit.edu/projects/from-value-to-vision-reimagining-the-possible-with-data-analytics/

Klaus, L. (2023). Marketing Automation – So sieht das perfekte Prozessmodell zur Implementierung aus. In U. Seebacher (Ed.), *Praxishandbuch B2B-Marketing: Neueste Konzepte, Strategien und Technologien sowie praxiserprobte Vorgehensmodelle – mit 14 Fallstudien* (pp. 435–454). Springer Fachmedien. https://doi.org/10.1007/978-3-658-40037-8_13

Körner, A. (2021). Roadmap zur Marketing Automation. In U. Hannig (Ed.), *Marketing und Sales Automation: Grundlagen – Umsetzung – Anwendungen* (pp. 61–78). Springer Fachmedien. https://doi.org/10.1007/978-3-658-21688-7_5

Kotler, P., Rackham, N., & Krishnaswamy, S. (2006). Ending the war between Sales & Marketing. *Harvard Business Review, 84*(7–8), 1–14.

Krieger, D. (2021). Entschlüsselung der Kunden DNA. In U. Hannig (Ed.), *Marketing und Sales Automation: Grundlagen – Umsetzung – Anwendungen* (pp. 149–158). Springer Fachmedien. https://doi.org/10.1007/978-3-658-21688-7_11

Kuckartz, U., & Rädiker, S. (2024). *Qualitative Inhaltsanalyse. Methoden, Praxis, Umsetzung mit Software und künstlicher Intelligenz* (6th ed.). Beltz Juventa.

Kurtzke, S., & Setkute, J. (2021). Analytics Capability in Marketing Education: A Practice-Informed Model. *Journal of Marketing Education, 1*(19). https://doi.org/10.1177/02734753211042404

Lammenett, E. (2024). Das Online-Marketing von morgen: Marketing-Automation, Marketing-Suites, künstliche Intelligenz und kanalübergreifende Strategien. In E. Lammenett (Ed.), *Praxiswissen Online-Marketing: Affiliate-, Influencer-, Content-, Social-Media-, Amazon-, Voice-, B2B-, Sprachassistenten- und E-Mail-Marketing, Google Ads, SEO, künstliche Intelligenz* (pp. 635–648). Springer Fachmedien. https://doi.org/10.1007/978-3-658-43610-0_24

Länsipuro, H., & Karjaluoto, H. (2021). Data-driven marketing processes: Boundaries and how to overcome them. In O. Niininen (Ed.), *Contemporary Issues in Digital Marketing* (pp. 22–31). Routledge.

Latinovic, Z., & Chatterjee, S. C. (2022). Achieving the promise of AI and ML in delivering economic and relational customer value in B2B. *Journal of Business Research, 144*, 966–974. https://doi.org/10.1016/j.jbusres.2022.01.052

Lepenioti, K., Bousdekis, A., Apostolou, D., & Mentzas, G. (2020). Prescriptive analytics: Literature review and research challenges. *International Journal of Information Management, 50*, 57–70. https://doi.org/10.1016/j.ijinfomgt.2019.04.003

Lilien, G. L. (2016). The B2B Knowledge Gap. *International Journal of Research in Marketing, 33*(3), 543–556. https://doi.org/10.1016/j.ijresmar.2016.01.003

Linneberg, M. S., & Korsgaard, S. (2019). Coding qualitative data: A synthesis guiding the novice. *Qualitative Research Journal, 19*(3), 259–270. https://doi.org/10.1108/QRJ-12-2018-0012

Lundin, L., & Kindström, D. (2023). Digitalizing customer journeys in B2B markets. *Journal of Business Research, 157*. https://doi.org/10.1016/j.jbusres.2022.113639

Maechler, N., Poenaru, A., Schulze, P., & Rüdt von Collenberg, T. (2017). *Finding the right digital balance in B2B customer experience*. McKinsey & Company.

Mattos, D., Casais, B., & Braga, A. (2021). Marketing Automation in Business-to-Business Relationships and the Emerged Value Cocreation. In V. Ratten & P. Thaichon (Eds.), *COVID-19, Technology and Marketing: Moving Forward and the New Normal* (pp. 85–99). Springer Nature. https://doi.org/10.1007/978-981-16-1442-2_5

MAXQDA. (n. d.). *MAXQDA*. MAXQDA. Retrieved January 5, 2025, from https://www.maxqda.com/de/

Mayer, H. O. (2012). *Interview und schriftliche Befragung: Grundlagen und Methoden empirischer Sozialforschung*. Oldenbourg Wissenschaftsverlag. https://doi.org/10.1524/9783486717624

McMullin, C. (2023). Transcription and Qualitative Methods: Implications for Third Sector Research. *VOLUNTAS: International Journal of Voluntary and Nonprofit Organizations, 34*(1), 140–153. https://doi.org/10.1007/s11266-021-00400-3

Mero, J., Tarkiainen, A., & Tobon, J. (2020). Effectual and causal reasoning in the adoption of marketing automation. *Industrial Marketing Management, 86*, 212–222. https://doi.org/10.1016/j.indmarman.2019.12.008

Misoch, S. (2019). *Qualitative Interviews*. De Gruyter Oldenbourg. https://doi.org/10.1515/9783110545982

Monat, J. P. (2011). Industrial sales lead conversion modeling. *Marketing Intelligence & Planning*, *29*(2), 178–194. https://doi.org/10.1108/02634501111117610

Nair, D., Sharma, A., Nair, R., & Bose, M. (2020). Enhancing Sales Efficiency: Leveraging Random Forest and Logistic Regression for AI-Powered Lead Scoring and Qualification. *International Journal of AI Advancements*, *9*(4), Article 4. https://www.ijoaia.com/index.php/v1/article/view/5

Nair, K., & Gupta, R. (2021). Application of AI technology in modern digital marketing environment. *World Journal of Entrepreneurship, Management and Sustainable Development*, *17*(3), 318–328. https://doi.org/10.1108/WJEMSD-08-2020-0099

Neumüller, K., & Bigliel, T. (2023). A Glance at the "Drop-Outs." In G. Schuster & B. Wecke (Eds.), *Marketingtechnologien: Innovative Unternehmenspraxis: Insights, Strategien und Impulse* (pp. 241–254). Springer Fachmedien. https://doi.org/10.1007/978-3-658-42294-3_17

Nygård, R., & Mezei, J. (2020). Automating Lead Scoring with Machine Learning: An Experimental Study. *Proceedings of the 53rd Hawaii International Conference on System Sciences*, 1439–1448. http://hdl.handle.net/10125/63916

Ohiomah, A. A., Benyoucef, M., & Andreev, P. (2016). Driving Inside Sales Performance with Lead Management Systems: A Conceptual Model. *Journal of Information Systems Applied Research*, *9*(1), 4.

Ohiomah, A., Andreev, P., Benyoucef, M., & Hood, D. (2019). The role of lead management systems in inside sales performance. *Journal of Business Research*, *102*, 163–177. https://doi.org/10.1016/j.jbusres.2019.05.018

Oliva, R. A. (2006). The three key linkages: Improving the connections between marketing and sales. *Journal of Business & Industrial Marketing*, *21*(6), 395–398. https://doi.org/10.1108/08858620610690155

Paschen, J., Wilson, M., & Ferreira, J. J. (2020). Collaborative intelligence: How human and artificial intelligence create value along the B2B sales funnel. *Business Horizons*, *63*(3), 403–414. https://doi.org/10.1016/j.bushor.2020.01.003

Philipp, M. (2021). Vom E-Mail-Marketing zum Lead Management. In U. Hannig (Ed.), *Marketing und Sales Automation: Grundlagen – Umsetzung – Anwendungen* (pp. 193–213). Springer Fachmedien. https://doi.org/10.1007/978-3-658-21688-7_14

Posluschny, P. (2025). Instrumente der kontinuierlichen Prozessverbesserung. In P. Posluschny (Ed.), *Qualitätsmanagement für Führungskräfte: Instrumente, Methoden, qualitätssichernde Maßnahmen* (pp. 67–78). Springer Fachmedien. https://doi.org/10.1007/978-3-658-46701-2_3

Przyborski, A., & Wohlrab-Sahr, M. (2021). *Qualitative Sozialforschung: Ein Arbeitsbuch* (5th ed.). De Gruyter Oldenbourg. https://doi.org/10.1515/9783110710663

Rackley, J. (2015). *Marketing Analytics Roadmap: Methods, Metrics, and Tools*. Apress. https://doi.org/10.1007/978-1-4842-0259-3

Radchenko, M. (2024, December 6). *Your Guide on How to Implement GDPR in Salesforce in 2025*. https://www.sfapps.info/how-to-implement-salesforce-gdpr-compliance/

Rainsberger, L. (2022). *AI—The new intelligence in sales: Tools, applications and potentials of Artificial Intelligence*. Springer Fachmedien. https://doi.org/10.1007/978-3-658-38251-3

Redding, S. (2015). Can marketing automation be the glue that helps align sales and marketing? *Journal of Direct, Data and Digital Marketing Practice, 16*(4), 260–265. https://doi.org/10.1057/dddmp.2015.27

Reklaitis, K., & Pileliene, L. (2019). Principle Differences between B2B and B2C Marketing Communication Processes. *Management of Organizations: Systematic Research, 81*(1), 73–86. https://doi.org/10.1515/mosr-2019-0005

Rosário, A. T., & Dias, J. C. (2023). How has data-driven marketing evolved: Challenges and opportunities with emerging technologies. *International Journal of Information Management Data Insights, 3*(2). https://doi.org/10.1016/j.jjimei.2023.100203

Rougemont, F., & Terstiege, M. (2022). Marketingautomatisierung in der B2B-Branche. In M. Terstiege, M. Cinar, & J. Hehemann (Eds.), *Marketing-Automation – Erfolgsmodelle aus Forschung und Praxis: Konzepte, Instrumente und Strategien für die Implementierung* (pp. 111–130). Springer Fachmedien. https://doi.org/10.1007/978-3-658-35823-5_8

Rustholllkarhu, S., Toukola, S., Aarikka-Stenroos, L., & Mahlamäki, T. (2022). Managing B2B customer journeys in digital era: Four management activities with artificial intelligence-empowered tools. *Industrial Marketing Management, 104*, 241–257. https://doi.org/10.1016/j.indmarman.2022.04.014

Sabnis, G., Chatterjee, S. C., Grewal, R., & Lilien, G. L. (2013). The Sales Lead Black Hole: On Sales Reps' Follow-Up of Marketing Leads. *Journal of Marketing, 77*(1), 52–67. https://doi.org/10.1509/jm.10.0047

Salesforce. (n. d.). *Smarter marketing automation on the world's #1 CRM.* Salesforce. Retrieved May 1, 2025, from https://www.salesforce.com/eu/marketing/automation/

Schreier, M. (2014). Varianten qualitativer Inhaltsanalyse: Ein Wegweiser im Dickicht der Begrifflichkeiten. *Forum Qualitative Sozialforschung / Forum: Qualitative Social Research, 15*(1). https://doi.org/10.17169/fqs-15.1.2043

Schuster, N. (2021). Marketing Automation ändert den Vertrieb. In U. Hannig (Ed.), *Marketing und Sales Automation: Grundlagen – Umsetzung – Anwendungen* (pp. 105–119). Springer Fachmedien. https://doi.org/10.1007/978-3-658-21688-7_8

Schuster, N. (2022). *Digitalisierung in Marketing und Vertrieb: Richtige Strategien entwickeln und Potentiale der Digitalisierung für mehr Umsatz nutzen.* Haufe. https://doi.org/10.34157/9783648158661

Seebacher, U. (2023). Das B2B Marketing Öko-System – Eine Reise durch die bunte Welt der B2B Begriffe. In U. Seebacher (Ed.), *Praxishandbuch B2B-Marketing: Neueste Konzepte, Strategien und Technologien sowie praxiserprobte Vorgehensmodelle – mit 14 Fallstudien* (pp. 53–101). Springer Fachmedien. https://doi.org/10.1007/978-3-658-40037-8_3

Sharma, K. K., Tomar, M., & Tadimarri, A. (2023). Optimizing Sales Funnel Efficiency: Deep Learning Techniques for Lead Scoring. *Journal of Knowledge Learning and Science Technology, 2*(2), 261–274. https://doi.org/10.60087/jklst.vol2.n2.p274

Silva, S. C., Corbo, L., Vlačić, B., & Fernandes, M. (2021). Marketing accountability and marketing automation: Evidence from Portugal. *EuroMed Journal of Business, 18*(1), 145–164. https://doi.org/10.1108/EMJB-11-2020-0117

Stamann, C., Janssen, M., & Schreier, M. (2016). Qualitative Inhaltsanalyse – Versuch einer Begriffsbestimmung und Systematisierung. *Forum Qualitative Sozialforschung / Forum: Qualitative Social Research, 17*(3). https://doi.org/10.17169/fqs-17.3.2581

Steuernagel, A. (2021). *Digitale Transformation des Marketings und Vertriebs in B2B-Unternehmen: Konzepte und Anwendungsbeispiele.* Springer Fachmedien. https://doi.org/10.1007/978-3-658-34889-2

Stevens, R. (2012). *Maximizing Lead Generation: The Complete Guide for B2B Marketers.* Pearson Education.

Świeczak, W., & Łukowski, W. (2016). Lead generation strategy as a multichannel mechanism of growth of a modern enterprise. *Marketing of Scientific and Research Organizations, 21*(3), 105–140. https://doi.org/10.14611/minib.21.09.2016.11

Tableau. (n. d.). *Vanity Metrics: Definition & How To Identify Them.* Retrieved June 2, 2025, from https://www.tableau.com/learn/articles/vanity-metrics

Terho, H., Mero, J., Siutla, L., & Jaakkola, E. (2022). Digital content marketing in business markets: Activities, consequences, and contingencies along the customer journey. *Industrial Marketing Management, 105*, 294–310. https://doi.org/10.1016/j.indmarman.2022.06.006

Terho, H., Salonen, A., & Yrjänen, M. (2023). Toward a contextualized understanding of inside sales: The role of sales development in effective lead funnel management. *Journal of Business & Industrial Marketing, 38*(2), 337–352. https://doi.org/10.1108/JBIM-12-2021-0596

Terstiege, M. (2022). Trends in der Marketingautomatisierung. In M. Terstiege, M. Cinar, & J. Hehemann (Eds.), *Marketing-Automation – Erfolgsmodelle aus Forschung und Praxis: Konzepte, Instrumente und Strategien für die Implementierung* (pp. 69–82). Springer Fachmedien. https://doi.org/10.1007/978-3-658-35823-5_6

Terstiege, M., Alexander, T., Cinar, M., & Pleißner, B. (2021). Marketer-Experteninterviews zum Einfluss von KI. In M. Terstiege (Ed.), *KI in Marketing & Sales – Erfolgsmodelle aus Forschung und Praxis: Konzepte und Instrumente zum erfolgreichen Einsatz künstlicher Intelligenz* (pp. 17–42). Springer Fachmedien. https://doi.org/10.1007/978-3-658-31519-1_2

von dem Berge, B. (2020). Teilstandardisierte Experteninterviews. In M. Tausendpfund (Ed.), *Fortgeschrittene Analyseverfahren in den Sozialwissenschaften: Ein Überblick* (pp. 275–300). Springer Fachmedien. https://doi.org/10.1007/978-3-658-30237-5_9

von Focht, T. (2022). Marketing Analytics – Technologien und Tools. In M. Halfmann & K. Schüller (Eds.), *Marketing Analytics: Perspektiven – Technologien – Anwendungsfelder* (pp. 75–103). Springer Fachmedien. https://doi.org/10.1007/978-3-658-33809-1_5

Vossebein, U., Hildmann, G., & Wengler, S. (2024). *Lead-Management: Prozesse – Menschen – Daten.* Springer Fachmedien. https://doi.org/10.1007/978-3-658-44535-5

Wedel, M., & Kannan, P. K. (2016). Marketing Analytics for Data-Rich Environments. *Journal of Marketing, 80*(6), 97–121. https://doi.org/10.1509/jm.15.0413

Wenger, S. (2023). Erfolgreiches Lead Management – Nothing's Gonna Stop us Now. In U. Seebacher (Ed.), *Praxishandbuch B2B-Marketing: Neueste Konzepte, Strategien und Technologien sowie praxiserprobte Vorgehensmodelle – mit 14 Fallstudien* (pp. 479–506). Springer Fachmedien. https://doi.org/10.1007/978-3-658-40037-8_15

Woelke, A. (2021). Zusammenspiel von Lead Management und CRM entlang der Customer Journey. In U. Hannig (Ed.), *Marketing und Sales Automation: Grundlagen – Umsetzung – Anwendungen* (pp. 215–223). Springer Fachmedien. https://doi.org/10.1007/978-3-658-21688-7_15

Wollin-Giering, S., Hoffmann, M., Höfting, J., & Ventzke, C. (2024). Automatic Transcription of English and German Qualitative Interviews. *Forum Qualitative Sozialforschung / Forum: Qualitative Social Research, 25*(1). https://doi.org/10.17169/fqs-25.1.4129

Wu, M., Andreev, P., & Benyoucef, M. (2024a). Smart Sales: Amplifying the Power of Predictive Lead Scoring in B2B Sales. *PACIS 2024 Proceedings*. https://aisel.aisnet.org/pacis2024/track09_digittrans/track09_digittrans/3

Wu, M., Andreev, P., & Benyoucef, M. (2024b). The state of lead scoring models and their impact on sales performance. *Information Technology and Management*, *25*(1), 69–98. https://doi.org/10.1007/s10799-023-00388-w

Zumstein, D., Oswald, C., Gasser, M., Mäder, L., Thüring, U., Völk, K., Merdzanovic, A., & Hannich, F. (2023). *Marketing Automation Report 2023. Den Automatisierung-Reifegrad messen und erhöhen* [Eine Studie des E-Commerce Labs]. ZHAW School of Management and Law. https://www.zhaw.ch/storage/sml/upload/Marketing-Automation-Report-2023.pdf

Zumstein, D., Rettenmund, M., Gasser, M., Cantin, V., Thüring, U., & Kölle, D. (2024). *Marketing Automation & AI Report 2024: Taktiken & Tools der KI-basierten Leadgenerierung* [Eine Studie der ZHAW]. ZHAW School of Management and Law. https://digitalcollection.zhaw.ch/handle/11475/30619

GPSR Compliance
The European Union's (EU) General Product Safety Regulation (GPSR) is a set of rules that requires consumer products to be safe and our obligations to ensure this.

If you have any concerns about our products, you can contact us on

ProductSafety@springernature.com

In case Publisher is established outside the EU, the EU authorized representative is:

Springer Nature Customer Service Center GmbH
Europaplatz 3
69115 Heidelberg, Germany

www.ingramcontent.com/pod-product-compliance
Ingram Content Group UK Ltd.
Pitfield, Milton Keynes, MK11 3LW, UK
UKHW041853290926
476121UK00001B/1
* 9 7 8 3 6 5 8 5 0 9 5 8 3 *